Frederic David Mocatta

The Jews of Spain and Portugal and the Inquisition

Frederic David Mocatta

The Jews of Spain and Portugal and the Inquisition

ISBN/EAN: 9783337245733

Printed in Europe, USA, Canada, Australia, Japan

Cover: Foto ©ninafisch / pixelio.de

More available books at **www.hansebooks.com**

THE

JEWS OF SPAIN AND PORTUGAL

AND

THE INQUISITION

LONDON : PRINTED BY
SPOTTISWOODE AND CO., NEW-STREET SQUARE
AND PARLIAMENT STREET

THE

JEWS OF SPAIN AND PORTUGAL

AND

THE INQUISITION

BY

FREDERIC DAVID MOCATTA

LONDON

LONGMANS, GREEN, AND CO.

1877

PREFACE.

THE following little sketch was originally composed as a lecture to some Jewish working-men at the East end of London. The subject is, to me, naturally an interesting one no less from a national than from a family point of view; I hope the Essay may also prove of some general interest. The position of the Jews in Spain and Portugal during a great part of the middle ages forms an exceptionally bright spot in their dark and chequered history, and developed some striking intellectual and moral features in an age when a great part of what now constitutes Civilisation was wrapped in mental darkness. The favoured position of the Jews in the Peninsula induced a vast Hebrew population to settle there; and although it became evident, after a time, that their prosperity, attracting, as it did, the jealousy of the bulk of people, would lead to their ultimate ruin, this could only be effected in a long and gradual manner, and could only be consummated by a cruel and violent measure—their forced expulsion.

The struggles of the Mohammedans and the Christians for supremacy had for centuries excited the minds of the Spaniards, and imbued them with a crusading spirit which would tolerate no dissidence in matters of religion; and this feeling was easily worked upon by the clergy, in regard to a numerous and thriving community, which remained utterly without the pale of the Christian Church.

Measures of restriction were followed by efforts at conversion on a scale of unprecedented magnitude, till such efforts grew into a persecution, and, still failing to attain the desired end, culminated in the edict of banishment.

Had the Jews possessed more tact during the earlier stages of their troubles, and adhered more closely to their scientific and literary pursuits than to the acquisition of wealth, they might probably have retarded, and possibly have averted, the final doom. It is, however, hardly likely that a population of little less than a million Jews would ever have been allowed to dwell in peace in a land ruled by monarchs as bigoted as Philip II. and his successors, and which almost till our own times permitted a court as arbitrary and as cruel as the Inquisition to hold an undisputed sway. The installation of this Tribunal under Ferdinand and Isabella forms an epoch in the history of Spain, and weighing as an incubus on all freedom of thought and action, was one of the main causes of the decadence of that great country, the effects of which are now so sadly visible. In expelling the Jews, Spain gave the greatest blow to her commerce, as in driving out the Mohammedans she did to her agriculture. Thus, the effects of bigotry and intolerance have recoiled with more lasting evils on the persecutors than on the persecuted; and Spain and Portugal languish, while more tolerant lands have flourished and are continually acquiring strength.

The following are the principal sources from which I have derived my facts:—

GRAETZ. ' Geschichte der Juden.'
KAYSERLING. ' Geschichte der Juden in Portugal.'
KAYSERLING. ' Ein Feiertag in Madrid.'
LINDO. ' History of the Jews in Spain and Portugal.'
LLORENTE. ' Historia de la Inquisicion de España.'
HERCOLANO. ' Da origem e establecimento da Inquisição em Portugal.'
AMADOR DE LOS RIOS. ' Estudios sobre los Judios en España.'
AMADOR DE LOS RIOS. ' Historia de los Judios en España,' vols. I. and II.

BEDARRIDE. ' Les Juifs en France, en Italie, et en Espagne.'
ANONYMOUS (NIETO). "Procedimiento de las Inquisiciones
    en España y Portugal,' etc., etc.

The subject is one which is capable of very considerable elaboration, both as concerns the position
and history of the Jews in the Peninsula, and the
workings of the Inquisition itself; and I feel that I
have rendered but very scant and imperfect justice
to a theme at once so interesting and so instructive.
I must therefore crave the indulgence of the reader
for putting before him a sketch so incomplete, my
only excuse being the very limited knowledge of the
subject which is generally possessed.

F. D. MOCATTA.

LONDON : *March* 1877.

THE JEWS OF SPAIN AND PORTUGAL

AND

THE INQUISITION.

———•◦•———

THE period when Jewish settlers were first attracted to the Iberian Peninsula, where they afterwards attained so high a position in learning and in wealth, and where for some centuries they so thoroughly acclimatised themselves as almost to forget their captivity and to regard themselves as in a new Judæa, is so remote, that no reliable historical data exist on the subject.

No doubt the Phœnicians, at a very early period, traded with the various ports on the Mediterranean, and, as is well known, the Carthaginians—a people closely allied to them in race, and both to them and to the Hebrews in language—founded several cities, and established colonies on the coast. This may probably have given rise to the tradition that Jews were already settled in the Peninsula in the days of Solomon, and that the Tarshish of the Bible was identical with the Tartessus of the ancients, a district of Southern Spain, the principal city of which was Gades, the modern Cadiz. It was also stated that Nebuchadnezzar made conquests in Spain, and sent captives from the vanquished kingdom of Judah to colonise them. These legends, fanciful as they are, and entirely unworthy of credence, were studiously kept alive by the Spanish Jews of later times. Certain it is, however, that Jews very early found their way to the Peninsula, and that when, on the fall of the Roman Empire, the Goths and Vandals conquered the country, large numbers of them were already established in various districts throughout the land.

Even under Roman rule the first restrictions against the Jews were promulgated at the Council held at Elvira (Iliberis), near Cordova, soon after the year 300, but the general confusion which followed the irruption of the barbarians, and the toleration of the earlier Gothic kings, who were Arians, afforded a period of comparative repose for more than two centuries. When, however, at the end of the sixth century, the Roman Catholic form of Christianity became the recognised religion of Gothic Spain, fresh edicts of intolerance followed fast from the various Councils, held principally in Toledo, and soon after, we begin to hear of those forced, and consequently feigned, conversions which in later times led to such sad and disgraceful results. The persecutions became so frequent and so violent that large numbers of Jews from Southern Spain sought refuge on the African coast, and a good understanding arose between them and the Moors, which the latter used to their advantage when a little later they crossed the Straits and invaded the Peninsula. The first successful irruption of the Moslems took place in 711, and such was the impetuosity of their onslaught, and the disorganisation of the Gothic states, that in less than five years the whole of Spain and Portugal was subjected to their rule. No doubt the sympathies of the Jews, oppressed and hunted down under the Goths, were strongly in favour of the invaders, to whom they were moreover allied by a kindred monotheistic principle, and a common Semitic race. At first but tacit spectators of the struggle, they were soon sufficiently admitted into the confidence of the Moslems to be entrusted with the garrisoning of Seville, Granada, and other large towns; they were also allowed a perfect toleration in the exercise of their religion. It is asserted, but without sufficient proof, that the Jews opened the gates of Toledo to the invaders while its defenders were occupied in celebrating a procession, on Palm

Sunday, in 712. At any rate, it is certain that the forced converts to Christianity at once returned to their old faith, and that large numbers of other Jews followed in the wake of the Moslem hosts, and vastly swelled the Hebrew population of the Peninsula. Once established on Spanish soil, they firmly retained their footing, even when, after the lapse of a few generations, a considerable territory had been reconquered from the Mohammedans by Christian valour. Communities of Jews not only flourished in all the more important towns of Spain and Portugal, but also established themselves north of the Pyrenees throughout the South of France. The new conquests of the Moslems were at first subjected to the Arab Caliphs of Damascus, but about the year 750, profiting by a revolution in the eastern capital, 'Abd-er-Rahman I. succeeded in establishing his independence, and governed the country with great wisdom and moderation. This monarch founded the University of Cordova, which in the course of a few generations became, with the schools of Seville, Granada, and Lucena, established by his successors 'Abd-er-Rahman II. and III., the great seats of the learning of the day. In order to shed additional lustre round his new foundation, 'Abd-er-Rahman encouraged and invited the presence of numerous

Jewish scholars, who were not slow to avail themselves of the advantages offered. The Jews, notwithstanding the downfall of their nationality, had
preserved their intellectual vigour through the constant and assiduous study of the law of Moses. In
the course of this, they had elaborated the vast
codex of the Talmud, on which they piled commentary after commentary, holding philosophical disputations on almost every subject relating to physical
science, civil polity, and social economy. These
studies, which saved the Hebrew people from lapsing
into that state of mental atrophy which characterised
what are usually called ' the dark ages,' were carried
on in the colleges, which they had, in the first
centuries of the Christian era, founded in Palestine,
Persia, and Egypt. The persecutions which raged
in Alexandria, and the fanatical outbursts which
followed the sudden rise of Islamism, had forced the
Jews to close these cherished abodes of learning, and
they were therefore naturally only too pleased to
flock to the new establishments where they had so
valuable an opportunity both of acquiring and of
disseminating knowledge. The Moorish rulers who
succeeded 'Abd-er-Ra*h*man I. were equally favourable
to Jewish scholars, and so much interest was excited
by Hebrew literature, that by command of Caliph

Hakim, about the end of the tenth century, Rabbi Joseph Ibn-Abitur Santos translated the whole of the Mishnah into Arabic. It would appear, by the names which are left on record, that by far the greater number of those who distinguished themselves in these centres of learning belonged to the Hebrew race. Numerous Jews attained high honour and lasting fame as poets, philosophers, astronomers, physicians, mathematicians, and grammarians, and many through their linguistic skill rendered an invaluable service to science and literature, by translating the classical authors of antiquity into Arabic, while they handed over to the Western world the treasures of Eastern lore, thus uniting the whole into one common heritage of human knowledge.

It is a very remarkable fact that, whatever branch of science or literature was cultivated by the learned Jews of these ages, the study of their scriptures, and of their ancient traditional writings which explained and illustrated them, always formed the basis of their mental operations. Deeply versed in Hebrew, the Jewish authors and poets of the eleventh, twelfth, and thirteenth centuries resuscitated the language of their ancestors, and numerous treatises on religious subjects, on philosophy, medicine, and general science

were produced in classical prose; whilst touching
and beautiful hymns and odes in verse rivalled, in
loftiness of conception and in elegance of diction,
the best periods of biblical composition. Thus for
fully four centuries flourished in Spain, Portugal,
and Southern France, a long list of distinguished
Jewish authors, writing on a great variety of subjects,
generally in Hebrew, but frequently also in Arabic.
The abstruse philosophy of that age has long since
given place to more practical studies, and the
languages employed are too little known in Europe
for the mass of these works to be in any way familiar
even to scholars of our own days. Moreover, in
after ages of bigotry and persecution, a large number
of the writings of these learned Hebrews were
wantonly given over to destruction, both in the East
and West, as being the productions of a hated and
heretical race, so that many of them have been
totally lost. Several of the poetical compositions,
however, still survive in the Jewish liturgy, and are
charming no less from the soul-stirring depth of
feeling which pervades them, than from the elegance of their versification and their purity of
diction.

It may not be out of place here to name a very
few of the more prominent of those distinguished

men, who illustrated not less the race to which they belonged, than the age and countries which gave them birth. Among such may be mentioned the poet and philosopher Solomon Ibn-Gebirol, in the eleventh century, the poet Jehudah ha-Levi in the twelfth, at which period also flourished the distinguished family of Ibn-'Ezra, many of whom held responsible positions in the State, and whose most remarkable member was the grammarian, commentator, and mathematician, Abraham Ibn-'Ezra, who died in 1194. The same century produced the well-known traveller Benjamin of Tudela, and the great Moses-ben-Maimon, or Maimonides. This extraordinary man (born at Cordova, 1135; died at Fostat, near Cairo, 1204), remarkable alike as philosopher, physician, astronomer, or commentator, is perhaps the greatest illustration produced throughout the middle ages, in any nation, or of any creed. His writings, which are voluminous, and are some in Arabic, and some in Hebrew, exercised a marked determination in forming the mind of his contemporaries, and established a lasting influence on his co-religionists, who have expressed the estimation in which they hold him, in the proverb, 'from Moses till Moses, there never was one like Moses.'

In the twelfth and thirteenth centuries flourished in Southern France the illustrious family of grammarians, the Kimchis, of whom the best known is David, who died in 1235. Rabbi Moses ben Nachman, or Nachmanides, also in the thirteenth century, was distinguished as a commentator and physician, and Alfonso X. of Castile, surnamed 'the Wise,' who laid the basis of a new system of astronomy, chiefly availed himself in his researches of the services of Jewish savants, whom he took pleasure in rallying round him.

In the course of a few centuries the Moors were gradually forced to give up.the greater part of their conquests in the Peninsula, first the Northern portions, then Toledo, the whole of Portugal, Valencia, Majorca, Seville, and Cordova, so that they retained, from the middle of the thirteenth to the close of the fifteenth centuries, nothing more than the Kingdom of Granada. At this period a Hebrew population, probably exceeding a million, and forming nearly an eighth of the whole inhabitants, was scattered over the land. This vast aggregate of the Jewish race not only included men foremost in literature and science, and especially valuable from their skill in medicine, but also all those who were best fitted for trade and commerce, and who understood almost by intuition the then little-known rules of finance, and the practical elements of political economy. The great nobles, who, being given up to plans of ambition and to martial pursuits, disdained the details of business, employed the Jews in the management of their vast estates, and thus frequently the thrifty vassals became the creditors to a large extent of their spendthrift lords. The clergy, too, very generally availed themselves of the services of Jews, as the administrators of the enormous landed endowments of which they were possessed, and the kings frequently conferred on them the office of Treasurer ; while almost all fiscal charges were confided to their care, and the collection of the taxes, which they usually farmed, was almost exclusively left in their hands.

It is true that the Jews laboured under certain disadvantages; that they had to pay a capitation-tax of thirty-four maravedis, or about eighteen pence, a year; that they were forbidden the use of arms; that they were compelled by law to inhabit a particular quarter of the town, and to wear a distinctive badge on their garments, provisions which, however, they often contrived to elude ; and also that, as time went on, restrictive enactments were multiplied and pressed more heavily upon them; but for all this, the Jews became vastly enriched, and acquired so large an amount of power in the State, that it would have been well-nigh impossible to have dispensed with their services. It may easily be imagined that an alien race, devoted to another creed, and possessing to a certain extent an autonomy of its own, a race too which, by its thrift and intelligence, knew how to attract to itself so large a portion of this world's material gifts, would in course of time become the object no less of the dislike than of the jealousy of the great bulk of the population.

The office of tax-collector, however properly administered, has never rendered those who held it very popular, more especially where it has been the practice to farm the taxes. The functions of the capitalist, too, may be indispensable in enabling various trades and enterprises to be carried out, but in circumstances where the lender had so slight a security that the legal rate of interest varied between 20 and 30 per cent., it is easy to understand how those who loaned out their capital could be stigmatised as usurers, and held up to the opprobrium of the very parties who availed themselves of their resources. Moreover, those who allow the accumulation of wealth to form the chief study of their lives, and who flourish on the needs of their neighbours, are sure to fall into a state of mental and moral degradation; and it is likely that the Jews of the Peninsula afforded much colour of truth to the allegation that they were grasping and avaricious. Their natural love of display also caused them, in defiance of sumptuary laws and popular prejudices, to indulge in splendour of domestic arrangements and costume, which still more excited against them the envy and jealousy of those by whom they were surrounded.

It is easy to imagine that the clergy were not slow to avail themselves of the growing unpopularity of the Hebrew race. The pulpits resounded with denunciations and menaces, laws of repression succeeded each other, and every inducement to conversion was offered. Sons of converted Jews were sure of promotion in the Church, then the great highway to all distinction and honour, and inheritance was by special enactments diverted from those who remained steadfast to their ancestral faith, for the benefit of such relatives as adopted the Christian tenets. Occasional outbursts, resulting in pillage and bloodshed, occurred from time to time, from the beginning of the fourteenth century. These hostile demonstrations, which it required all the force of the law to repress, became more violent in intensity, and of more constant recurrence, until they terminated in the final catastrophe of the expulsion.

In 1321 was organised a savage persecution in the South of France, under the name of the War of the Shepherds, which, spreading into Northern Spain, was only put down after much bloodshed by James II., of Aragon, chiefly by the arms of the Jews themselves. Soon after this that fearful pestilence called the Black Death, spreading from Asia, desolated every country throughout Europe, and the origin of the plague, being inscrutable, was assigned to the Jews, who, although as great sufferers as the rest of the community, were accused of having poisoned the wells. Nevertheless, the wealth and intelligence of the Hebrews in the Peninsula were so indispensable that they continued to enjoy the highest places in the State, which still protected their worship and legalised the profession of their faith.

Under Alphonso XI. (1312–1350) and his son Pedro, surnamed the Cruel (1350–1369), the Jews enjoyed great favour, and by the latter, Don Samuel Levi Abulafia was placed at the head of the finances and, surrounded by a number of subordinates of his own religion, faithfully performed the duties of his

trust. This officer was permitted to build, at his
own expense, the sumptuous synagogue at Toledo,
now the church of Nuestra Señora del Transito,
which still gives evidence no less of his munificence
than of his consummate taste. After having lived
in a state of unexampled magnificence, he at length
fell a victim to the envy which his ostentation and
pride had excited, and died in prison and under
torture in 1360.

Even Don Henry of Trastamare, who violently
wrested the sceptre from his half-brother Don Pedro,
found himself obliged to confide many of the highest
places of the crown to Jewish hands, and in the
neighbouring country, Portugal, the Jews were at
the very zenith of their power.

The greater, however, were the worldly fortunes
of the Hebrews, the more determined were the clergy
upon their fall, and finding that they could make
but little impression on the governing classes, they
allied themselves with the populace, on whose prejudices and superstitions it was by no means a difficult task to work. The denunciations from the
pulpit grew more frequent and more heated, the
populace became inflamed, and the Jewish quarters
forthwith presented scenes of havoc and bloodshed.
No accusation could be too absurd or too improbable

to obtain credence : at one time it was that the Jews had blasphemed by cutting in pieces the Host, or consecrated Wafer, when the blood was seen to issue from it, and pour down the streets; at another, it was asserted that they had betrayed mocking gestures while a religious procession was passing; whilst the most frequent and horrible accusation was, that they had stolen and murdered a Christian child for the purpose of celebrating their paschal rites. In consequence of all these allegations the sumptuary laws were again insisted on, obsolete edicts of restriction, dating from the period of the Gothic kings, were brought to light, and the Jews were kept in a constant state of terror, which made their lives a burden and a continual dread. It must be owned that among the Jews themselves a state of demoralisation had set in, and though the tales invented against them were no less improbable than impossible, it has been shown that their intense devotion to the pursuit of worldly gain had induced habits of ostentation, and much lowered their moral and intellectual status since the days of Maimonides, and of the scholars of Cordova and Seville. With the exception of medicine, of which the Jews held almost a monopoly for many centuries, and in which they were so distinguished that, amid the most violent persecutions, there was hardly a great personage of Church or State who did not employ the services of a Jewish physician, pure science was no longer cultivated. Philosophy and legitimate Hebrew literature had given place to the abstruse and often absurd mysticism of the Cabbala, and to the mazy subtleties of the Sohar; and poetry, no longer aspiring to the loftiest conceptions, and the greatest elegance, aimed chiefly at clever conceits, in which alliterations and acrostics seemed the highest end. Moreover, numerous men of worldly mind, seeing the horizon of their ambition limited by their religious profession, passed over to the dominant creed, generally entering the clerical career as the readiest road to preferment, and frequently becoming among the most hostile adversaries of their brethren in race. These men, armed with their previous knowledge of Judaism and of Hebrew lore, were employed to refute their former associates by means of their own weapons, and wove specious subtleties to prove that the dogmas of the Catholic Church were established no less by the Hebrew scriptures than by the Talmud itself. Towards the end of the fourteenth century it became the custom to hold religious disputations between the clergy (generally converted Jews) and the Rabbis, and, as is usual in such cases, neither side being convinced, the doubtful palm was always accorded to the stronger party, and the Jews were further stigmatised as obstinate adherents to a proven fallacy.[1]

The storm which was to culminate in the final expulsion of the Jews from the Peninsula was silently but surely gathering. Early in 1391 a fanatical archdeacon, named Martinez, fulminated a most tremendous diatribe against the Israelites in the public square in Seville; the populace, goaded to phrensy, rushed on the Jews' quarter, destroying, pillaging, and massacring in every direction, and when at last, by means of the strong arm of the law, the fury of the marauders was stayed, it was found that no less than 4,000 Jews had fallen victims in this barbarous onslaught. Hardly three months later the same horrid scenes were repeated, and this time with far more fearful results. The slaughter was about equally enormous; many succeeded in effecting their escape, whilst numbers were sold into slavery to the Moors, and multitudes sought safety by submitting to be baptised, so that of the

[1] It is said that these disputations were the cause which led the Jews to adopt the Christian mode of dividing the text of the Hebrew Scriptures into chapters and verses, for the purpose of reference, there being no such division in the original text.

30,000 Jewish inhabitants of Seville hardly any remained.

These terrible atrocities were repeated in numerous other towns throughout Spain—in Cordova, Burgos, Logroño, Barcelona, Gerona, the Island of Majorca, &c. In Gerona the Rabbis assumed a firm attitude, and counselled their brethren rather to abandon life than their ancestral faith ; in many places the congregations were fearfully reduced, and in others utterly rooted out. Numbers of Jews migrated into Portugal, where still for two or three generations they enjoyed rest and full toleration, while others sought refuge in the Moorish kingdom of Granada, where liberty of conscience existed to a great degree ; but many more ostensibly embraced Christianity, seeking under the shadow of the cross that protection for life, family, and possessions which as Jews could no longer be theirs. The precedent of persons who under violent persecution had outwardly simulated a change of religion, whilst privately following out their own faith, their belief in which remained unchanged, was by no means wanting in the Peninsula. At various periods numbers of Mohammedans had outwardly professed themselves Christians, returning to their own faith when the storm of persecution had passed, and in like manner Christians had often in appearance temporarily embraced Islam to tide over a period of fanaticism, whilst from time to time Jews had been forced on an emergency to put on the garb of either of the dominant creeds, without in any way giving up their inward convictions. Even the great Maimonides himself is said to have been compelled, while wandering in Morocco, to assume, with the rest of his family, the externals of Mohammedanism. His father had removed with his children to Fez, it is thought for the purpose of strengthening his afflicted brethren in their wavering constancy, the Moorish Jews being, at that time, subjected to a most galling persecution. At a later period, when the great philosopher was assailed for his conduct on this occasion, he thought fit to publish a statement, less as a vindication of his own action, than as a guide to other Jews, who might find themselves overwhelmed by a sudden persecution without having the means of escape. The whole story of Maimonides's simulation of Islamism is, however, entirely denied by many eminent Jewish writers, and by such the 'Iggereth-ha-Shemad,' or Letter on Apostasy, is considered as a spurious document.

Thus at this crisis arose groups of pseudo-converts, whose number, at first limited, became larger by every new outburst of persecution, till, in the

early part of the fifteenth century, they were esti-
mated at no less than 200,000. These ostensibly
converted Jews were called by their brethren in race
'Anusim,' or 'Forced,' and by the Christians
'Cristianos Nuevos,' or 'New Christians,' whilst
the populace branded them with the name of 'Marannos,' a word of uncertain derivation, probably a
corruption of 'Maranatha,' and signifying 'accursed.'

While things were in this state, towards the close
of the fourteenth and rise of the fifteenth century
appeared the Dominican monk Vincent Ferrer, afterwards canonised for the result of his missionary
labours. This wild fanatic, with a crucifix in one
hand, and a scroll of the Law of Moses in the other,
thundered out his arguments against the Jewish religion, holding forth sometimes in the open market-
places, sometimes in the churches, and not unfre-
quently in the very synagogues themselves. His
phrensied ravings terrified the Jews to the verge of
madness, and wrought the populace into so excited
a state that his discourses were rarely over before
the Jews' quarter became a scene of havoc, and
multitudes of terror-stricken Hebrews begged for
the waters of baptism to save them from imminent
destruction. The conversions effected in this manner
were really very considerable, but such was the

miraculous power with which the Fray Vicente was popularly endowed, that the wildest statements obtained easy credence. He is by some reported to have brought over no less than 35,000 Jews in Salamanca alone, in one year (1411); and it is seriously asserted that he effected 50,000 conversions during the quarter of a century of his preaching.

But St. Vincent Ferrer was not the only adversary to the Jews at this period. Another Dominican monk, Cardinal de Luna, assumed the Papal Tiara, under the name of Benedict XIII., and although he was never recognised as other than antipope by the mass of Christendom, he was supported in his pretensions by the kings of Aragon, and held his court in grand state at Tortosa in Catalonia from 1412 to 1417. In order to signalise his zeal, and to insure the support of the clergy, Benedict was violent in his hostility to the Jews. He and his confidential physician, a converted Jew, Joshua Lorqui, who had assumed at the font the name of Geronimo de Santa Fé, and who was a profound Talmudist, devised a grand disputation to be held in Tortosa in 1413. Sixteen learned rabbis were invited to argue on the tenets of Judaism, especially as regards the coming of the Messiah, with Geronimo, and some others, among whom was Andreas

Beltraço, another converted Jew, and almoner to the Pope, Benedict himself presiding over the conference. The proceedings were opened in grand state, with Pope and cardinals, and a vast assemblage of noble and learned auditors, and no less than sixty-nine sittings were held, extending over a period of eighteen months, Latin being the language employed. The first meetings maintained a show of calmness and dignity, but as time wore on, and it became evident that the arguments on the one side made no impression on the other, declamation and menace assumed the place of reasoning, and the conference broke up in the wildest disorder, it being finally ruled that the Talmud was a mass of blasphemy and heresy, which the Jews could no longer be permitted to use. A string of papal Bulls, offensive and oppressive to the last degree to the Hebrew race, immediately followed, and as a natural consequence a further large number of pretended conversions took place. At length in 1417 the great question of the papacy was set at rest, Benedict XIII. was deposed, deserted, and left to die in obscurity, and Martin V., a pontiff who appears to have been favourably inclined towards the Jews, was universally recognised as the successor of St. Peter. But the harmful influences thus powerfully set in motion could not be lulled to rest; the Church teemed with converts from Judaism, who sought to show their zeal by the oppression of their former brethren. Among these Paul de Sta. Maria, Bishop of Burgos, and his sons, one of whom was Bishop of Cartagena, and Alfonso de Espina, who became Rector of the University of Salamanca, notably distinguished themselves, and fanned the flame of persecution which the populace were only too ready to keep alive.

While matters were in this threatening position in Spain, alarming indications showed themselves in the western kingdom of the Peninsula. In Portugal the position of the Jews had hitherto been highly favoured; as in Spain, they were liable to certain disabilities which were not very rigorously enforced. They dwelt generally in separate quarters, and were nominally subject to sumptuary laws as to apparel, &c., but they were internally governed by their own regulations, their counsels being presided over by their Chief Rabbi, while frequently many of the highest offices in the State were confided to members of their body. The Chief Rabbi (*Arrabi-Mór*) was always appointed directly by the Crown, and so important was deemed the post that the filling-up of a vacancy in the office, which occurred in 1384, gave rise to a court intrigue, the effects of which exercised a lasting influence over the destinies of the country, and became the main cause of placing Don John of Aviz on the throne of Portugal, and averting the threatened fusion of that kingdom with Castile. The wealth and position of the Jews, added to their inordinate love of display and supercilious manners, had long rendered them unpopular, and the recent persecutions in Spain had tended to vastly increase their number in the sister country, whilst the clergy studiously favoured the growing aversion, which first terribly exploded in Lisbon in December, 1449. The outburst appears to have originated in a street riot, in which several Jews were insulted and maltreated, and on their offering resistance the mass of the populace precipitated itself on the Jews' quarter, crying out: 'Murder them, pillage them!' Acting in the spirit of their words, the rabble ransacked the whole district; many Jews were killed, and more were wounded, and it was only through the efforts of the military, and by the personal intervention of the king (Alfonso V.), who hurried to the capital, that order was at length restored. The condition of the Jews in Portugal was visibly growing worse, yet for more than forty years no open outburst of persecution is recorded, and many high offices still continued to be confided to them. The brothers Ibn

Jachia, who belonged to a long line of counsellors and physicians, still maintained those charges at the court of Alfonso V. Abraham de Beja and Joseph Zapateiro were commissioned to accompany the voyage of discovery to the East Indies; and the names of other Hebrews are also found in prominent places. Moreover, though the Jews of Portugal hardly attained as high a position in learning as their brethren in Spain, Hebrew literature was largely cultivated, and in the reign of John II., Hebrew printing was introduced into Portugal, and continued up to the year of the expulsion, exhibiting a very great perfection. But the man who shed the greatest lustre over the declining period of the Jews in the Peninsula was Don Isaac Abravanel (b. 1437, d. 1509), of a family which, descended from the royal house of David and lately immigrated from Spain, had already through several generations distinguished itself by its attainments, and was destined to enjoy in other lands an honourable succession for nearly a couple of centuries. This great man was for many years Minister of Finance, and confidential counsellor of the king. Endowed with wonderful mental abilities, and with a determination to achieve greatness, gifted by nature with a remarkable power of acquiring influence over other men, and with a rare desire to benefit others through his own advantages, Abravanel became no less the friend and adviser of his sovereign than of those royal and noble personages who formed the Court, avoiding with the rarest tact those difficulties and jealousies to which his exalted position rendered him eminently liable. Possessed of large wealth, he was munificent in acts of charity, a notable instance of which occurred on the taking of Arzila, a port on the African coast, by the Portuguese, on which occasion 250 Jewish captives were sold into slavery. Abravanel subscribed largely to purchase the freedom of these unfortunate persons, and collected from his wealthier brethren, both in Portugal and in other lands, sufficient funds not only to place them in liberty, but also to provide for their future necessities. Deeply imbued with the love of Hebrew literature, he gave up his hard-earned leisure to serious studies, and commenced amid the cares of business and the toils of State a learned commentary on the law of Moses, and other portions of the Bible, and several philosophical works, tasks which, carried on through all the vicissitudes of his career, were only brought to a close at a later period of his life, when exile gave him comparative repose. At the death of his great friend and protector, Alfonso V., in 1481, and the accession of his son John II., the whole of the courtiers of the late king were disgraced, and Abravanel with difficulty succeeded in eluding the pursuit of the new sovereign, who confiscated the whole of his vast estates. Reduced to poverty he managed to escape into Spain, where he joined Don Abraham Senior, the great farmer of taxes in Toledo, who admitted him into his partnership, and thus enabled him to re-construct his ruined fortune. He now pursued his studies with unremitting zeal, terminating some of his earlier works, and publishing some very original and valuable commentaries on the prophetical and historical books of the Bible. We shall presently see how he nobly came forward to endeavour to avert the doom of expulsion from his brethren in Spain, foiled in which he fled to Naples, where he was hospitably received by the King, Ferdinand I. On the death of this sovereign Abravanel accepted office under his son and successor Alfonso II., and when that prince was shortly afterwards forced, through the irruption of the French, to abdicate in favour of his son, and to flee to Sicily, he accompanied him thither. His family, however, were dispersed in flight, and the infant child of his eldest son Judah, himself a very distinguished man, was kidnapped by the King of Portugal, and forcibly brought up in the Christian faith. Alfonso died in 1495, when Isaac Abravanel fled to Corfu, whence he afterwards returned to Monopoli, near Bari, and finally betook himself with the remnant of his family to Venice, where he died in 1509. Meanwhile things were tending to a crisis in Spain, where edict followed edict, to embitter the lot of the Jews, and in 1474 Ferdinand and Isabella succeeded to the united crowns of Aragon and Castile. The creation of so important a monarchy inspired no less rulers than subjects with the dominant desire to bring under the same sceptre those provinces of southern Spain, which, though tributary since 1244, were still governed by the Mohammedan kings of Granada, and thus subjecting the whole country to Christian rule. The King was ambitious, unscrupulous and avaricious to the last degree; the Queen, though possessed of many womanly virtues, was superstitious, and entirely in the hands of the priests, and both entered warmly into the new crusade. At such a juncture, when religious feeling was so excited, it was not likely that the Hebrew race, as much an object of aversion from the obstinacy with which it rejected Christianity as of jealousy on account of the vast wealth which it had accumulated, would meet with much toleration. The sect of New Christians had been rapidly growing, and as it increased, the line of demarcation between them and the ' Old ' Christians had become more marked, so that it was now hard and fixed, and as it became evident that the Christianity of the neophytes was little more than a pretence, their condition was but slightly improved by their apparent conversion. It is true that the converts ostensibly conformed to the tenets of the Catholic faith, assuming fresh names, filling their houses with crucifixes, images of saints, and other symbols of Christianity, and regularly attending the services of the Church; but these new habits sat uneasily on them. It is by no means difficult to imagine that persons, brought up in a faith which they were forced to abandon through fear or worldly interest, would not in their hearts be very zealous in their attachment to the religion which they were constrained to adopt. In secret they observed as many of the practices of Judaism as they were able to do without fear of discovery, studiously inculcating Jewish notions into the minds of their children, and endeavouring by every means in their power to keep alive in their descendants the memory of the old religion. Thus they led, as it were, lives of perpetual deceit, and ill at ease within themselves, were ever silently praying that their conformity to practices, which appeared to their mind but little less than idolatry, might not be accounted to them as mortal sin. It was therefore, in a great number of cases, easy to obtain proofs that the New Christians were by no means purified from their old errors and superstitions, and thus their assumption of the dominant faith did not long shield them from the violence of the populace. Hence we hear of persecutions specially directed against the New Christians, in Valladolid, in 1470, in Cordova, in 1472, and so on, during the next twenty years, in various other towns.

The relations between the converts and their former co-religionists appear to have been of the most intimate nature : ties of blood, and feeling, and a strong bond of commercial interest, created a powerful link between those Hebrews who had placed themselves without the pale of Judaism, and those who still remained within. The latter appeared to recognise in the defection of the former the inevitable force of circumstances, and sought to aid the 'Anusim' by all means in their power, to keep up the clandestine exercise of such rites of Judaism as they still contrived to practise. Thus the Jews still more drew upon themselves the animadversion of the clergy, and gave rise to a future source of accusation, that of being guilty of ' Judaising,' for which they were about to suffer in a terrible manner.

Matters were evidently growing to a climax; and the materials for the great act of state-policy, which was to purge Spain from the stigma of Judaism, were only awaiting some bold master-hand to combine them and give them full force. Such soon arose in the person of Fray Tomas de Torquemada, a Dominican monk, who had been confessor to the Queen in her younger days, and who was possessed of an iron will, joined to great mental power, and an unflinching pertinacity of purpose. For the carrying out of his ideas, the creation of a great religious and political engine, which would become their legal embodiment, was absolutely necessary, and accordingly he laboured with all the energy of his nature to procure the establishment in Spain of the Court of the Inquisition. This tribunal had originally been devised to crush the heresy of the Albigenses early in the thirteenth century, by Fray Domingo de Guzman, better known as St. Domenic, who obtained from Pope Innocent III. (in 1212) the title of Inquisitor-General. It first began its career in Sicily, whence it shortly extended to other states of Italy, to Southern France, Catalonia, and afterwards to Aragon, in which kingdom from time to time

heretics were given over to the flames. Castile and
Portugal were also to some degree under its influence, but as the heresies which called it forth no
longer could be said to exist, and the Church of
Rome held undisputed sway over Western Christendom, the Inquisition, by the middle of the fifteenth
century, had become generally a languid institution,
and in most countries had already ceased to be.

It might easily have been thought that at the
period when the revival of letters, the invention of
printing, and the discovery of America gave a new
tone to human thought, and opened fresh avenues to
public and individual enterprise, this organisation
for diving into the minds of men and watching the
habits of their privacy, in order to guard against any
original speculation on matters of belief, would have
died out, scared away by the day-light of advancing
civilisation.   Unfortunately, the very reverse occurred, and the institution became re-organised and
intensified at the precise juncture when it might
naturally have been expected to become extinct.   It
so happened that in 1477 Philip de Berberis, Inquisitor of Sicily, which formed part of the dominions
of Ferdinand, came over to seek the confirmation of
a privilege accorded by the Emperor Frederic II., in
right of which one third of the possessions of con-

demned heretics became the property of the Inquisition; and this iniquitous system having received the royal sanction, it became evident how magnificent a prey would be ready to fall to a similar institution in Spain, could such but obtain a legal establishment. Fray Alonso de Hojeda, prior of the Dominican convent in Seville, and Nicholas Franco, the papal nuncio, exerted all their energies to this end, and succeeded in obtaining from Sixtus IV., in 1478, a Bull authorising Ferdinand and Isabella to choose sundry archbishops, bishops, and other persons, clerical and lay, for the purpose of conducting investigations in matters of faith, and proceeding against heretics and those who protected them. Ferdinand entered readily into a scheme which promised such brilliant results to his cupidity; but the Queen hesitated to sanction in Castile the establishment of a tribunal which not only threatened proceedings of a most vexatious and cruel character, but which was odious to the greater part of her subjects, and disliked even by a large portion of the clergy. It was at first sought to temporise; Cardinal Mendoza, Archbishop of Seville, published a special catechism for the use of the New Christians, and various other methods were adopted in order to avert the threatened crisis, but the Dominicans were not to be thwarted. Alonso de Hojeda, Fernando de Talavera, confessor of the Queen, and afterwards Archbishop of Granada, Diego de Merlo, Pedro de Solis, and other priestly personages in favour at Court, headed by Torquemada himself, whose influence was unbounded, never for a moment relaxed their energies. They constantly represented to her the wickedness of the ' evil seed of Israel,' the blasphemies they were ever uttering, the intrigues they were ever weaving, and the impiety they were ever practising under the veil and cover of their assumed Christianity.   Such arguments could not fail to triumph in the end, when addressed to a weak and superstitious woman like Isabella, and in September 1480 she reluctantly and tremblingly affixed her signature to the document which established the Inquisition in her dominions.   Soon afterwards Fray Tomas de Torquemada was created Inquisitor-General, the convent of St. Paul, to which was shortly added the castle of Triana, in Seville, was given up as the first seat of the Tribunal, and a field adjoining was appointed as a Quemadero, or burning-place for heretics, a spot marked by a square stone pavement, with a colossal statue of a prophet at each corner, and which retained its name down to the commencement of the present century.

The opening of the year 1481 saw the installation, in its more extended and terrible form, of that horrible court, which stands unequalled for acts of atrocity perpetrated in the name of religion, and which, under the pretext of purging Spain from heresy and Judaism, gradually involved the whole country in ruin, from which it has never been able to recover. Since the Church claimed no jurisdiction over acknowledged Mohammedans or Jews, and since accusations of heresy and witchcraft were at this period by no means frequent, the whole force of this new and tremendous engine was directed against the Marannos or New Christians. Frightened out of their senses by this terrible apparition, vast numbers of these unfortunate people fled from Seville, seeking refuge with the Duke of Medina Sidonia, the Marquis of Cadiz, and other great nobles, whose almost sovereign position in their various domains was thought to be able to afford protection from the impending storm. Hospitably received as they were, their flight proved of no avail, for the first edict of the new court was to summon all nobles, barons, and feudatories to send back all the fugitives to Seville within a fortnight, under pain of deprivation of their titles and honours, and sequestration of their estates. Within four days of the installation of the

Inquisition took place the first *auto-da-fé*, or Act of faith, when six persons perished in the flames. In March, April, and November followed fresh human sacrifices, to such an extent that, in the first year, 298 individuals were burned, and in the second, no less than 2,000; besides which 17,000 persons were subjected to do penance, involving either total or partial loss of their property, and the disgrace of themselves and their families.

The large scale of the proceedings of this second year (1482) was no doubt induced by an artful snare, devised by the Inquisitors to entrap the largest possible number of the converts. This was the issuing of an ' Act of Grace,' by which within thirty days all those New Christians, who had been guilty of practices denoting a relapse into Judaism, were summoned to come forward and declare themselves, and holding out the assurance of full absolution, and the preservation of their lives and property, to all such as were contrite and promised amendment.

Numbers of the unfortunate Marannos were lured by this ' Edict of Grace,' and consequently the Tribunal became possessed of a register of the suspected, which was indefinitely enlarged, as none who made confession were allowed to depart until they had given a list of all those of their relations or acquaintances who might possibly be guilty of a similar relapse,—a plan which afforded in many instances a fruitful means of gratifying private malice and personal vindictiveness. The individuals thus named were, on the expiration of the term of the ' Edict of Grace,' ordered to present themselves within six days, and if they refused to comply, they were taken by force from their houses and lodged in the dungeons of the Inquisition.

It is interesting to know what were considered as proofs .of a relapse into Judaism. Thirty-seven articles were drawn out, and the mention of a few of them is sufficient to prove how frivolous and absurd were the grounds, which sufficed to deprive multitudes of unfortunate fellow-creatures of happiness, property, and life. It was to be investigated whether an individual had made a difference between Saturday and other days, by laying a white cloth on the table, or putting on a clean shirt, or better clothes than on other days ; whether he had cut the throat of a fowl in killing it for food, or had withdrawn the sinew from an animal destroyed for the same purpose ; whether he had eaten meat during Lent, or on the Fasts prescribed by the Church, or had abstained from food on the Jewish day of Atonement, or other Hebrew Fasts, or had used baths, cut his hair, or pared his nails on days preceding such Fasts, or had eaten unleavened bread, or used certain herbs in Passover, or procured green branches, or made presents of fruit to friends at the time of the Feast of Tabernacles, or drunk 'Casher' wine, (that prepared for Jewish ceremonials,) or eaten meat killed by Jews, or repeated certain Jewish blessings on particular occasions, or recited the Psalms of David without concluding with the words 'Glory be to the Father, and to the Son, and to the Holy Ghost;' whether any parent had given Hebrew names to his children, or washed or shaved the head of a child on the part on which the chrism of baptism had been poured, or invited his friends and relations to dine before leaving on a long journey, or whether a dying man had turned his face to the wall, or had it so turned by others, or a dead body had been washed in warm water, or the water had been emptied out from all vessels in the house of a deceased person, together with a long catalogue of similar enquiries.

Such were among the proofs of relapse from the newly adopted faith into the errors of the old superstition. Sad indeed was the fate of those, of whom it could be pretended that they cooked their stews in oil instead of lard, and many Old Christians in after times had to repent that their casual dislike to pork or shell-fish had brought them under the suspicion of being secret votaries of what it pleased the Inquisitors to designate as 'the impious law of Moses.'

By such means and by the agency of the machinery which is about to be described, it is certainly not surprising that the victims of the Inquisition were no longer counted by hundreds, but by thousands, and tens of thousands, especially as the tribunal established in Seville was only the prototype of numerous other similar courts instituted in all the larger cities of Spain: Toledo, Cordova, Ciudad Real, Saragossa, Valencia, Barcelona, Madrid, Salamanca, Valladolid, Segovia, and various other places, all could boast of their courts of Inquisition, their dungeons, and their Quemaderos, which, established generally despite the most lively opposition of the inhabitants, grew to be regarded in after times as fixed institutions.

In Aragon the creation of the New Tribunal was so unpopular, that a plot was laid against the first inquisitor in Saragossa, Don Pedro de Arbues, who, though he was made aware of the conspiracy, and consequently wore armour beneath his clerical habit, was smitten down and killed in the cathedral of that city in September, 1485. As is the usual result of crimes of this description, a revulsion of feeling followed, with a persecution of the New Christians, who were accused of having instigated the deed. The Aragonese Inquisition became an accomplished fact, and the slain Inquisitor at a later period received the beatification of the Church.

It may easily be imagined how the new proceedings inspired fear far and wide, when it is considered that not only some hundreds of thousands of the population were known to belong to the New Christians, but also that by intermarriage with the converts vast numbers of the people, largely including the highest nobility and clergy, were the descendants of Jews, and were consequently amenable to the proceedings of the dreaded tribunal. Many of the more sober-minded Spaniards saw with horror the extent to which this abuse of power was carried, and, joining in a common protest, petitioned the Pope for a curtailment of the functions of the new magistrates ; the New Christians supported the petitioners by the more forcible arguments of their gold, and vast were the sums sacrificed to obtain Bulls for the mitigation of the severity of the courts. In the first instance the result was successful, and Sixtus IV. in 1482 issued a Bull blaming the indiscriminate zeal of the Inquisition; but Ferdinand was inexorable, and by means of lavish gifts he extorted from this Pope, and his successors Innocent VIII. and Alexander VI., fresh powers confirming the Tribunal in the full exercise of its office.

Anxious to give a precise legal embodiment to the institution, Torquemada and his associates drew up an elaborate code of twenty-eight articles, or constitutions, defining the duties and aims of the Holy Court in the following manner. After announcing the establishment of the Inquisition in Seville, and decreeing the institution of similar courts in various towns throughout the country, the Edict of Grace was set forth, inviting heretics and Judaisers within thirty days to come to declare themselves, and to denounce all others whom they knew to follow similar practices. Those who voluntarily came forward and confessed within this term were subjected to fines in money, and to the ceremony of a public absolution, which involved the deprivation of titles and honours, and rendered the absolved ineligible for all offices of public trust; a ' re-habilitation ' was, however, in some instances procurable at the expense of a large portion of their fortunes. No absolution was granted unless the persons who claimed it not only penitently confessed their transgressions, but also furnished a list of all those whom they believed to be guilty of similar relapses. Against all those who did not offer their confession within the thirty days assigned, the entire confiscation of their property was decreed. For this purpose their possessions were assessed, not at the date of their accusation, but at that of their assumed committal of the crime of heresy, so that if they had made them over to other hands, they were to be restored to the Inquisition. Persons under twenty years of age, who pleaded that they had been led into error by their parents or guardians, were to do penance by being condemned to wear during one or two years the disgraceful garb of the Sambenito, in which they were to appear in all church ceremonials.

The Sambenito (or saco bendito), which we shall often have occasion to mention, as figuring in acts of penance and in 'acts of faith,' was a cloak of coarse serge, which varied in form and in design at different periods. The garment covered the whole body, and was yellow in colour, with flames, demons, serpents, and crosses painted on it in red, and arranged according to the delinquency of the wearer. With the sambenito was worn the 'coroza,' or high-pointed cap, made of a like material, and covered with similar devices, and generally bearing on its front a placard, on which were written the name and offences of the wearer.

Those who were committed to the dungeons of the court with a view to their being handed over to the secular arm, for capital punishment, as impenitent, and who afterwards declared their repentance, obtained the commutation of their sentence to imprisonment for life in the cells of the Inquisition. Those who remained impenitent, or who relapsed from their penitence or were supposed to have made a feigned confession, were handed over to the secular arm to be committed to the flames. Such as refused to confess, or were suspected of having made only a partial confession, were to be subjected to torture, which was to be administered under the eyes of two Inquisitors, or, where such could not attend, of their appointed delegates, who were to conduct the interrogations, and to take down the depositions of the accused. In cases where such confessions were afterwards retracted, as naturally often happened, a fresh application of torture might be made, and though this second infliction was at a later period pronounced illegal, the effect was the same, since the procedure was merely declared to be 'suspended,' and the prisoner was subjected to its continuation at a subsequent period. Those who, being accused,

were able to elude the officers of the tribunal, were
considered condemned by default, and were deprived
of their property, and often burned in effigy. A
deceased person, against whom an act of heresy
could be proved at any period subsequent to 1479,
was condemned to have his body exhumed and
burned, and all the property he had left was to be
taken from those who had inherited it, provision
only being made in these, as in other cases of confiscation, that children under age, who were thus
disinherited, should be brought up on some small
provision allowed by the State, and duly educated in
the Catholic faith. All inheritances derived from
persons who had incurred condemnation were declared invalid and forfeited to the Crown. The Inquisition claimed full jurisdiction over all seignorial
domains, as well as over the Crown lands, and was
free to form such establishments as it deemed necessary throughout the whole country. Lastly followed
certain clauses concerning the discipline of the Inquisitors themselves, adjuring them to live in peace with
each other, prohibiting them from receiving presents
or bribes, and enjoining that all disputes which might
occur between them were to be settled in secret
by the Inquisitor-General, without reference to the
bishop of the diocese or to the ecclesiastical courts.

Besides the foregoing, eleven additional acts were promulgated relating to the internal government of the tribunal, defining the duties of the Inquisitor-General, of the various Inquisitors throughout the provinces, of the registrars, secretaries, legal officers, alguazils, and of the vast assemblage of subordinate officers, who were afterwards known as the 'familiars of the Holy Office.' Moreover, a resident at the Court of Rome was appointed to represent the Inquisition at the Papal See.

Such form the bases of the constitution of that celebrated tribunal which was, for more than three centuries, to place its iron hoof on the liberties of the nation, crushing out all freedom of human thought, and reducing the minds of men to one dead level of stagnant uniformity. With so terrible an engine invented specially for their destruction, it is not wonderful that the New Christians should become panic-stricken, and, leaving their homes in despair, should seek refuge in other lands. Their former Hebrew brethren in faith, trembling for their own fate, liberally assisted them for this purpose, and tens of thousands poured out of Spain, the greater part flocking into Portugal, many into the still Mohammedan kingdom of Granada, while others sought a refuge in Italy, and even in Rome itself.

But since the year 1481, Ferdinand and Isabella had been strenuously prosecuting their campaign against the Moors in the south, and at length, after more than ten years of arduous struggle, the war ended in the triumph of the Christian arms; the Moorish King, Abdallah or Boabdil, submitted, his capital, Granada, surrendered, and by the opening of 1492 the Moslem rule in the Peninsula had disappeared for ever, and Ferdinand and Isabella became undisputed monarchs of the whole of Spain.

While the sovereigns, elated with their recent success, were still at Granada, surveying from the Alhambra the crests of the snowy Sierra, with the fertile Vega at its base, and the rich and vast territory which they had won, no less for themselves than for Christendom, the Inquisitors brought to bear on them all the sophistry of their arguments to carry out at this favourable juncture the long conceived and desired project of the expulsion of the Jews from Spain. The plan was by no means without a precedent; in 1290 Edward I. had, without consulting parliament, banished the Jews from England; in 1306 Philippe le Bel pronounced their first expulsion from France, their final exile, after having been recalled, being effected by Charles VI. in 1394; they had been also expelled at various periods from most of the states of Northern Italy, and from Sicily, as also from various states of Germany.

The Hebrew race, as has been seen, had very long been an object of intense jealousy and superstitious aversion in Spain, and probably the popular antipathy, coupled with the anticipation of the speedy reversion to themselves of the huge wealth of the Jews, which it would be quite impossible that they could carry away with them, acted as powerful incentives towards the consummation of the measure. Torquemada, as may readily be supposed, was an earnest supporter of the project; his wrath had always been rabid against the insincerity of the New Christians, and the secret communications which they maintained with the Jews had further incensed him against the hated race. Moreover, he had recently insisted on the deposition of two bishops, sons of converted Jews, because they had refused to authorise the bodies of their fathers to be taken from their graves, upon a demand which had been made under the pretext that they had died in heresy. He had also attempted to compel the Rabbis of Toledo to give up upon oath the names of all those converts to Christianity who still practised Hebrew rites, a demand which was boldly refused.

In order to prevent all connivance between the
Jews and the Converts, Torquemado made a firm
resolution never to cease from his efforts till he had
succeeded in the design of driving all the former
from the realm, a project in which he found but
little resistance from Ferdinand. That prince,
though mainly relying upon Jewish capital for the
prosecution of his wars against the Moors, had never
disguised his antipathy to the Hebrew race. On the
taking of Malaga in 1487 he had caused twelve New
Christians who had fled thither and resumed their
old faith to be transfixed with lances, and had sold
450 Jewish captives, mostly women, into slavery,
from which they were nobly ransomed by Don
Abraham Senior for the sum of 20,000 doblas of
gold. The assent of Isabella was less easy to obtain,
for she always evinced an under-current of feeling
which made her at first recoil from sanctioning acts
of cruel and oppressive persecution.

The force of bigotry and fear, and the distorted
reasoning of the Inquisitors, proved however too
strong for any sentiment of compassion, and on
March 31, 1492, went forth the fatal edict enjoining
that all non-baptised Jews must quit the whole of
the Spanish dominions, including the islands of
Sicily and Sardinia, within the space of four months.

The proclamation was based entirely on the grounds that the Jews were proved guilty by the Inquisitors and others of perverting Christians to their own belief, and spreading among them the knowledge and practice of Jewish rites and ceremonies. It stated that originally it had been contemplated to limit the measure to the expulsion of the Jews from all the cities and places in Andalusia, but that it had been found necessary to extend it to the whole country. Despite the ordinances which had been passed for preventing communication between Jews and Christians throughout the land, the former had continued to use every means in their power to subvert the holy Catholic faith by endeavouring to bring over faithful Christians to the observances of the law of Moses. It was thus deemed absolutely imperative, after mature deliberation, to banish the Jews from the whole kingdom, and accordingly they were all ordered to depart, never to return, before the end of the month of July in the current year, 1492. All such as remained after that date incurred the penalty of death, and of confiscation of their entire property to the royal treasury. All persons, of whatever rank, who harboured any Jew or Jewess after that date, were to forfeit their estates or property. The edict concluded by a promise of royal protection to the

E

Jews during the remaining four months, with permission to travel in safety, and to sell, alienate, or otherwise dispose of all their moveable or immoveable property. They were also to be allowed to export their wealth and substance either by sea or land, with the exception of gold, silver, or other articles prohibited by law.

It may be deemed highly creditable to the Jews that the accusations brought against them were strictly limited to their wishing to bring over Christians to Judaism, a charge which could only have been meant to apply to the New Christians, who were in reality Jews themselves. The then prevalent and favourite accusations that the Hebrews were given to practices of usury and false dealing, that they had abducted and crucified Christian children, had desecrated the Host, or had poisoned large numbers of the population in the course of their extensive medical practice, might, not unnaturally, have been expected to find a place in the document; to none of these subjects, however, was the slightest allusion made, although the Inquisitors were industrious in circulating all these charges in justification of the measure.

This remarkable and final edict, although it might have been seen looming in the distance for many years, fell like a thunder-bolt on the Jews. To be forced to quit the soil which their ancestors had inhabited for so many centuries, which they loved as no other land had been loved by Israelites since the destruction of Jerusalem, to abandon those many relatives, who though they had nominally quitted their faith, still remained Jews in feeling, and who were now to be handed over to a ruthless persecution, to exchange the wealth which they had so long enjoyed for poverty and exile, was too bitter a thought for endurance. Great was the interest used, and vast were the efforts made to avert the fatal decree. The Jews offered to submit to any terms, and to sacrifice any amount of treasure, merely to be permitted to remain on Spanish soil.

At this crisis that grand and remarkable character, Don Isaac Abravanel, who, as we have seen, had long been established at Toledo, stepped boldly forward, and accompanied by some of the more notable of his co-religionists, threw himself at the feet of the King and Queen, offering to raise 300,000 ducats, provided the degree were revoked. It is stated that the arguments he used were so cogent, that the royal pair were on the point of consenting, when Torquemada rushed into the royal presence with a crucifix in his hand, and thrusting it before

the sovereigns, exclaimed : 'Judas Iscariot sold his
master for thirty pieces of silver; you wish to sell
him for 300,000 ducats; here he is, take him and
sell him.' This concluded the argument; the fate
of the Spanish Jews was now irrevocably sealed. In
proportion as the day of their departure drew near,
and the means of realisation became more difficult,
their anxiety to dispose of their worldly goods grew
greater; valuable plots of land were sold for a few
pieces of cloth, fine houses were exchanged for a
couple of mules, and in many cases the riches of the
Israelites melted away into those few articles, which
they could carry with them, and the beasts, which
were to transport them. Moreover, the convents and
public institutions, the nobles, and persons of every
class, were largely indebted to the Jews, and as no
provision was made for the collection of the debts
becoming due to them after the date of their enforced departure, their losses from this source were
almost incalculable, and the gain to the debtors was
of course proportionately enormous. Despite the
edict, saddles and furniture were stuffed full of gold
pieces, while such as could succeed in transmuting
their money into bills of exchange, which were not
then very general in Spain, did so on any terms,
however ruinous.

Sad and harrowing were the scenes presented in these last days of sojourn in Spain. In most communities visits were paid by the Jews to the tombs of their ancestors, to which they bade a long farewell. In Plasencia the Jews made over to the city their cemetery and a considerable tract of adjoining land, under condition that their burial-ground should never be built over; in Vitoria a similar compact was arranged, and in Segovia amid tears and lamentations they removed many of the tomb-stones of their fathers, and carried them with them in their long wanderings. During the whole of that sad month of July were to be seen, along the high-roads of Spain, the long files of the Hebrew people, downcast and sorrowful, some in the decrepitude of age, others in the tenderness of youth, the sick, and the halt, the infirm and the weak, included in the common fate. The outcasts wended their weary way under a scorching sun, toiling over the arid, dusty plains, and the rugged mountains, and through the rocky defiles which characterise the Peninsula, conveying with them the scrolls of their holy law, and the few remnants of their wrecked fortunes, and frequently casting a lingering look back towards those dear homes which they were never to see again. The mocking gestures of the peasantry and

townsmen, as they passed along, the contempt and
scorn which they met with on every side, made these
melancholy processions still more painful, and at
length by the first days of August the exodus was
completed, and the doom was fulfilled. By a strange
coincidence the 2nd of August 1492 fell upon the
9th Ab, 5252, A.M., and this anniversary of the
destruction of the first and of the second temples,
and of so many troubles to the House of Israel, had
never recurred before with such sad reality as on
the present occasion. The number of Jews who thus
quitted Spain has never been ascertained; Mariana
puts it as high as 800,000, whilst some other his-
torians estimate it as low as 160,000; so that taking
a middle course we may probably assume it to have
been little short of 400,000.

The fate of the exiles was varied in the different
lands where they sought refuge. Those who escaped
to Morocco and Algiers found an inhospitable reception; many were sold into slavery, some starved
to death, whilst others were ripped open in the
hopes of finding gold pieces in their bodies, and a
few preferred to return to Spain and receive baptism,
a fate which was forced on some others, who were
wrecked on the Spanish coast. In Turkey they were
well received, and Sultan Bajazet is said to have

remarked: 'A politic king, indeed, must be this Don Fernando, who impoverishes his kingdom to enrich our own.' In Italy, though Genoa would only allow them to remain three days, they found in most states permission to abide, and in some, as in Naples, they received a hearty welcome; into Navarre some few were admitted, but only to await in a couple of years an entire expulsion with the rest of their brethren. The major part emigrated to Portugal, the aged and noble Rabbi and great Talmudist, Isaac Aboab of Toledo, having obtained, despite much opposition, the permission of King John II. to their entering the country, though only in consideration of each immigrant paying a capitation-tax, and on the understanding that within eight months they should leave the country, for which purpose proper ships should be provided by the government at moderate rates of passage-money. Indeed, it appears that the Portuguese Jews themselves were alarmed at this enormous immigration of their brethren. Their own position was at this period by no means assured, and so sudden an increase of their number, composed of persons mostly in distressed circumstances, was naturally calculated to create the most anxious misgivings. Nevertheless, it is stated (though there are great discrepancies as to numbers), that nearly 150,000 of those expelled from Spain availed themselves of this temporary refuge.

A remarkable fact connected with this expulsion was the firm attitude of the Rabbis, who everywhere counselled steadfastness and resignation; people bowed down by suffering passively submitted to their doom, and thus, though some few Jews, and among them Abraham Senior and his son, preferred conversion to banishment, the total number who rather submitted to baptism than to exile was quite insignificant. The fires and terrors of the Inquisition had already sufficiently proved that conversion afforded but slight guarantee for safety, and that New Christians were but little more free from persecution than had been those who had not abandoned the faith of their fathers.

Thus was Spain deprived of her large Jewish population; the synagogues were purified and used as Christian churches; the vast sums of money which were owed to the Jews, and the still larger amounts which they were forced to leave behind them, found their way partly into the hands of their debtors, or still more into those of the sovereign; the chief professors of medicine were sent out of the country, to the terrible inconvenience of the population, and trade and industry languished till they almost died out.

Unfortunately at the time of the expulsion the plague was raging in Castile, and the fugitives brought with them the disease, propagating it wherever they went, and not unnaturally causing their advent to be viewed with loathing and horror. This circumstance induced King John to hasten their departure from Portugal, for which purpose ships were duly provided according to the agreement, but such was the temper of the captains and sailors, that they subjected the Jews to the hardest possible conditions; they plundered them of their goods and valuables even to their very clothes, and landed them naked and bare of everything on barren points of the African coast, leaving them to die of starvation or to be sold into slavery to the Moors. Nor was this all: the King wrested from their parents all children between the ages of three and ten of those Jèwish immigrants who from poverty or otherwise had omitted to pay the capitation-tax on entering, or who were forced to remain in Portugal, and had them transported to the newly discovered Islands of St. Thomas, which then swarmed with alligators and other beasts of prey, to be brought up as Christians. Six hundred of the richest families of the Spanish

Jews, .however, had by a separate transaction procured for themselves the right of remaining in Portugal, on payment of 60,000 gold cousados, and a
few useful mechanics were also exempted from the
action of the general decree.

These painful proceedings on the part of the King
of Portugal lead us to consider the state of the
indigenous Jewish population in that country. We
have seen the high position which they had occupied
for many centuries ; how they had held charge of the
greatest trust ; how they had farmed the revenues
of both Church and State, in the exercise of which
office, though bringing on themselves the animadversion of the populace, they had been found to be more
liberal than Christian collectors, and how until 1449
few or no attempts at persecution had been made.
As has been related, Alfonso V., who reigned from
1438 to 1481, and who was principally engaged in his
African campaigns, employed many Jews in places
of high trust, and was generally favourable to them.
It is true that during the latter part of this reign,
and in the succeeding one, jealousy and bigotry were
steadily growing, that edicts had been passed con-
fining the Jews more severely to their own quarters,
prohibiting them from having Christian servants,
from wearing silk or jewels, or using plate, or riding

on horses, edicts which must have been especially galling to persons used to a splendid mode of life, and fond to excess of display, but for all this, they were tolerated. Their worship and observances were recognised by the law, and beyond the privileges largely conceded to converts, one of which, highly immoral in its tendency, was, that any child of Jewish parents, who became a Christian in their lifetime, was to take immediate inheritance, as though the parents were already dead, their religion was not interfered with.

Alfonso's successor, John II., notwithstanding his barbarous treatment of the unfortunate Jewish fugitives from Spain, firmly resisted the introduction of the Inquisition, neither was he disposed to expel a population, whose wealth and intelligence were eminently useful; but the horrible cruelties he had perpetrated, and the persecuting spirit he had displayed, could not fail to have a fearful influence on the minds of the people in regard to the native Jews of Portugal. The bitterness of feeling which had been growing for many generations was gathering to a climax, when in 1495 Don John died, and his only legitimate son, Don Alfonso, having been killed by a fall from his horse four years before, his cousin, Don Manoel, ascended the throne.

This prince, whose success in his various enterprises and discoveries won for him the appellation of
the 'Fortunate,' commenced his reign by evincing
the most tolerant spirit. He revoked the oppressive
edicts of his predecessor, and restored the Jews to
the position they had held before, trusting rather to
obtain their conversion by mildness and mercy, than
by harshness and compulsion. The Hebrews sought
to show their gratitude by the offer of a large sum
of money, which the King refused to accept. A
learned astronomer, who in those days passed also
for an astrologer, by name Abraham Çacuto, was
consulted by Don Manoel on every great occasion,
and other learned Jews enjoyed his protection and
support. This was however but a transient gleam
of sunshine, and the storm soon gathered more
darkly than before. Don Manoel had hardly been
a year on the throne when he sought the hand of
Donna Isabella, the young widow of the late crown-
prince Alfonso, and the eldest daughter of Ferdinand
and Isabella. Whether he was smitten by the charms
of the princess, or whether the alliance with her
opened out to his ambition the vista of the eventual
union of the two crowns of Spain and Portugal on
his own head, and on that of his progeny, the
Catholic sovereigns having but one son, has never

been proved, but certain it is, he was excessively ardent in his suit.

The princess inheriting to a marked degree the bigotry of her parents, absolutely refused to listen to the addresses of Don Manoel, unless that prince consented to banish from his dominions all Mohammedans and Jews. With regard to the former, of whom no very large number still remained in Portugal, it was agreed that their forced conversion would lead to reprisals on the many Christians who were scattered through Moslem States, and therefore it was decided to limit their penalties to expulsion, every facility being granted for their leaving the country; whilst the Jews, who had no means whatever of recrimination, were to be dealt with according to the pleasure of the sovereign. It was for many months debated whether the elimination of so large a number of the wealthiest and most industrious of the population could be effected without causing a national misfortune, and on the other hand the more moderate among the clergy submitted that baptism received under compulsion possessed no power of salvation, and was therefore inoperative; but the King was deaf to all these arguments. In December 1496, Don Manoel issued a proclamation ordering that all non-converted Jews should leave Portugal within ten months under pain of confiscation of property, which was to fall to those who informed against all such as should disobey. Those who agreed to depart were to have powers afforded them of collecting their debts, and realising their property; they were also to have means of transport duly provided. But this was not all; in the following April appeared another edict ordaining that all the children under fourteen of those who had chosen exile rather than conversion, should be forcibly taken from their parents, and being distributed through the whole country, should be handed over to persons, who should bring them up in the Christian faith. This barbarous edict was to be carried out at the approaching Feast of Passover, which all Jews celebrate together in family groups.

The state of desperation and agony into which the Jews were plunged is hardly to be imagined. Multitudes of children were hidden away by their parents, and many were concealed by the more merciful among the Christians, but all these were diligently sought out, dragged forth, and forced to the font, while many instances occurred in which maddened fathers and mothers first destroyed their offspring with their own hands, and then committed suicide.

During the few months which remained to them, the Jews tried every means in their power to soften the heart of the King, and lastly finding all efforts without avail, they sought to be allowed three points from which they might make their exit, instead of the one sole port, which had been allotted. After dallying with them for some time, Don Manoel informed them that only one place of departure could be assigned, and that was Lisbon itself. More than 20,000 Jews under these circumstances assembled in the capital, and were lodged in a vast barrack called the Estáos, where every means of fair promise and foul intimidation was employed to make them renounce their faith. A fresh edict now went forth that all children between fourteen and twenty should also be taken from their parents and baptized, and multitudes were dragged forcibly by their hair and by their arms into the churches, and compelled to receive the waters of baptism, together with new names, being afterwards given over to those who undertook to instruct them in the Catholic faith. Next the parents themselves were seized, and were offered to have their children restored to them, if they would consent to be converted; in case of their refusal they were to be placed in confinement for three days without food or drink. It is indeed

wonderful that any mortals could be proof against
so terrible and fiendish an ordeal; yet to the glory
of the Hebrew race very many still remained un-
moved. Resistance was, however, not to be tolerated,
and it was therefore decreed that the same fate was
to be meted out tó the adults and to the aged, as
had already been the portion of the younger members
of the race of Israel. Amid the most heart-rending
cries and the most determined resistance, men and
women in the flower of their days, or the decrepitude
of age, were dragged into the churches, and forcibly
baptized amid the mocking and exultation of an
excited populace. But seven or eight of the whole
number of those who maintained their constancy,
succeeded in eluding force, and managed to secure
a passage to the coast of Africa.

The Jews who were still scattered through other
parts of the country, seeing the fate of their brethren,
were forced to assume the garb of Christianity, many
seeking in a self-inflicted death the only refuge from
apostasy, and thus, nominally, was Judaism extin-
guished in Portugal, as it had been five years before
in Spain.

Amid these horrors and barbarities were celebrated the nuptials of Don Manoel and Donna Isabel,
but the union was of short duration; the princess

died in little more than a year, following to the tomb her brother Don John, the only son of Ferdinand and Isabella, and later on the King married her sister Donna Maria. The wily monarch, who by such absolute and ruthless acts had complied with the conditions of the princess and her bigoted parents, and had thus managed ostensibly to purge the land from Judaism and Mohammedanism without conceding the establishment of the Inquisition, despite all the powerful interest which had been brought to bear upon him to that end, now sought by outward acts of conciliation and mildness to reconcile the New Christians to the religion they had been forced to adopt. Later in the year 1497 appeared an edict by which the converts from Judaism were shielded from persecution for the next twenty years, during which time every means was to be provided for instructing them in their new faith. At the end of this period all difference between Old and New Christians was to cease. Those then accused of Jewish practices were to be handed over to the civil law, and if found guilty were to be punished with the confiscation of their property, which was to fall to the next Christian heir. The population, however, were not to be satisfied with this mild treatment of the Hebrew race, and the hatred they

F

bore to the converts was, if possible, more deadly than that which they had manifested while they openly remained Jews. Restriction followed restriction, till the position of the New Christians became so intolerable, that large numbers sought refuge, after disposing of their worldly goods, by emigrating to other lands; but to the great majority this course was evidently impossible.

The Spanish monarchs continued to work vigorously to induce their son-in-law to allow the introduction of the Inquisition into his dominions; but all they could obtain was a law which prohibited any Spaniard from fixing his residence in Portugal, unless he could show that he had not been guilty of any offence against religion. This law, however, was quite inoperative, and numbers of New Christians from Spain, terrified by the proceedings of the Inquisition, still continued to cross the frontier, adding thereby to the popular outcry. In 1503 a famine, and in 1504 a riot in the streets of Lisbon, gave rise to outbursts of the rage of the populace, and in 1506 the plague further worked up the feelings of the multitude. On Whitsunday of this year, whilst the congregation were supplicating for a deliverance from the scourge in one of the principal churches, the reflection of light from a crystal covering the

Host above a crucifix caused the excited populace to cry out, 'A miracle, a miracle!' The effulgence was evidently but the play of light, and one of those present, unfortunately a New Christian, was heard to observe that he could see nothing remarkable in the appearance.

Those near him, hearing the observation, rushed on the unfortunate man, killing him on the spot, and burning his body on a pile heaped up in a moment in the public square. Soon the whole city was in an uproar, and the air was rent with cries of 'Heresy, heresy!' The populace seized hold of all the New Christians they could find, indiscriminately slaying among the number many Old Christians, who were thought to have Jewish features, destroyed and pillaged houses, and gave over the capital to scenes of havoc and destruction. Men, women, and children were dragged from the churches, where many had sought refuge, and burnt alive in the public streets, and it was only at the end of the third day, when more than 3,000 persons had been sacrificed to the popular fury, that the tardy intervention of the law managed to secure a semblance of order.

Don Manoel, incensed at these rabid persecutions, sought to reassure the New Christians by a fresh edict, by which he granted them full equality before the law, and extended their term for thoroughly instructing themselves in the tenets of the Christian faith till the year 1526. It was furthermore ordained that all New Christians were at liberty to leave the country if they pleased, whilst those who had already quitted, were assured that they would be unmolested if they chose to return.

During the remainder of this reign, which closed in 1521, it does not appear that the converts suffered any violent persecution, though the feeling towards them but little improved. The new King, John III. (1521–1557), was possessed with the most intense hatred of the Jewish race; nevertheless, urged by the ministers of his father, he began his reign with a semblance of toleration, and promised the New Christians a prolongation of their time of sufferance till 1534.

And now recommenced in earnest the intrigues for the establishment of the Inquisition in Portugal. A converted Jew, named Henriquez Nunez, surnamed, from his orthodox Catholic practices, 'Firma-fé,' wormed himself into the confidence of his former brethren in faith, and making use of the secrets thus treacherously obtained, conveyed to the King the alarming fact that the greater part of the New Christians were still entirely Jews at heart, and bore but the outward semblance of their adopted faith. He therefore strongly urged the institution of the Tribunal, which in Spain had proved so eminently useful in detecting and eradicating heresy. This man was stabbed to death in 1524,—a deed which was visited with terrible consequences on the New Christians. Neither the Pope nor the Portuguese clergy, nor even the mass of the people, viewed with much satisfaction the institution of the Inquisition; but the Queen, a sister of Charles V., that powerful monarch himself, and the Dominican monks, were untiring in their efforts, and in December, 1531, Clement VII. issued a Bull for the establishment of the Tribunal in Portugal. For ten years, however, the matter was kept pending; the New Christians were naturally horror-stricken, and vast sums of Jewish gold found their way to the treasury of St. Peter, to endeavour to avert the threatened doom. Among other means they maintained a secret envoy at Rome, a converted Jew named Duarte da Paz, high in the confidence of the King; but in 1539 this man, who only worked for his personal interests, found it to his advantage to denounce the proceedings of the New Christians to Don John. It happened, however, that Duarte had incurred the suspicion of the Pope; he was thrown into prison, and on his liberation he fled into Turkey, and there died as a Mohammedan.

Many were the plots and counter-plots, the Bulls and Counter-Bulls, till at last, in 1541, the Court of the Inquisition began its terrible career in Lisbon, and the first *auto-da-fé* was celebrated there in October of that year. One final effort was made in 1519 by the Jews to procure their readmission into Spain, when on the accession of Charles V. (First, of Spain) to the throne, an important deputation of Marannos waited upon him in Flanders, and offered the sum of 800,000 gold ducats, provided he would grant them permission to return, with the free exercise of their religion. The monarch, who was at the time hardly pressed for money, showed every sign of yielding, but Cardinal Ximenes, who after the death of Deza, the successor of Torquemada, had become Inquisitor-General, despatched an envoy to Brussels, begging the Emperor to desist from a transaction by which the interests of the faith were to be bartered away for vile lucre.

Thus in the middle of the sixteenth century, the golden age of modern art, the flourishing period of newly-revived literature, when the rough habits, engendered by constant turmoil and discord, were giving place to milder manners, the awful spectre of the Inquisition became a living reality in the whole breadth of the Peninsula, and throughout those enormous colonies in America, in Africa, and in Asia, which were subject to the crowns of Spain and Portugal. There is little doubt that the recent birth of Protestantism, which threatened to overwhelm the whole of Roman Catholic Christendom, and which gave so vast an amount of trouble to the Emperor Charles V. in his German and Flemish dominions, strengthened the hold of the Inquisition in Spain, and operated largely in procuring its establishment in Portugal. As, however, the new doctrines found but little favour in either country, the weight of its terrors fell principally on the Jews, its machinery being also often artfully adapted, so as to draw within its meshes all individuals who were in any degree deemed by the Holy Court to be obnoxious, but whose position rendered them difficult to deal with by any other process.

Even cardinals and bishops, and the princes and princesses of the royal house, did not escape without incurring the censure of the Tribunal, and the unfortunate Don Carlos, Philip II.'s only son then living, was probably a victim to its machinations. Prominent political personages and ministers of state were particularly amenable to the suspicion of

the Inquisition, and all those in authority, whom it
in any way desired to remove, were sure to fall into
its grasp, and to be crushed within its fearful fangs.
Thus it became a gigantic engine no less politically
than socially, and assuming to control the religious
life of men, grew to be in reality the most vital, or
rather the most deadly organ of the State. The
press too was subjected to the control of the holy
office, and thus through the aid of the strictest cen-
sorship it stifled scientific investigation and original
thought, and made itself master of every avenue of
the human mind. The system of delation and secret
information was so subtle and so widely spread, that
no person, whatever might be his condition, or however orthodox might be his practice, was free from
incurring suspicion. The most elaborate method of
espionage was devised, children were encouraged to
reveal the private practices of their parents, servants
were invited to divulge the secrets of the closet,
workmen were enticed to denounce the procedure of
their employers, and the domesticity of the family
was unveiled by every possible artifice. Thus
mutual confidence between man and man was closed
up; reticence and deception took the place of
brotherly intercourse and good fellowship, and a
sullen reserve begotten by suspicion and fear reigned

through the whole of society, and in time assumed the form of a national characteristic.

In order to extend the working of the Tribunal over as wide a field as possible, anonymous declarations were accepted as valid, and many were induced to betray others in the hope of thereby avoiding suspicion for themselves, while private enmity and malice found no easier manner of gratification than by handing over the enemy to the tender mercies of the Holy Court. The suspected were seized without notice, and dragged, often from their beds, from their family circle, to be lodged in the dungeons of the Inquisition. Family and friends were neither allowed to know the charges preferred against the prisoner, nor to hold any communication with him, and thus wives frequently found themselves in a moment condemned to widowhood, and children to orphanage, without knowing the fate of the dear one so ruthlessly snatched from their embrace. Long years of anxiety and watchfulness, of painful expectation and wearing uncertainty, tediously passed away, and when such prisoners as obtained a pardon came forth, and were restored to their families, their sickened forms and emaciated frames long betokened the treatment to which they had been subjected. Moreover, through the remainder of their lives they

were ever afterwards zealously watched, as a 'relapse' was never forgiven.

The course of legal procedure was arranged in
such a manner as to leave it entirely in the power of
the judges to establish the guilt or innocence of the
accused. Prisoners were to be 'admonished' on
each of the first three days of their imprisonment,
and in urging them to confess, the Inquisition lost
no opportunity of asserting that voluntary penitents
would be mildly dealt with. As the accused were
never informed who were the parties who denounced
them, or what formed the leading points of accusation, it was rare that confessions either of innocence
or guilt proved satisfactory to the judges. If at the
end of these admonitions and examinations no satisfactory result could be arrived at, a paper compiled
by the Inquisitors, and setting forth the nature of
the accusations, together with a number of other
crimes, of which the prisoner had never been really
accused, was handed to him, and an advocate from
among the legal officers of the court was, if desired,
placed at his disposal. As, however, the accused
could only communicate with his counsel in the
presence of the Inquisitors and the registrar, this
advantage proved entirely nugatory, and the prisoner
was remanded and committed anew to his cell, either

for a future interrogation, which might be delayed for weeks, months, or, even as was often the case, for years, or else in order to be dragged forth again to submit to torture, by which means it was hoped to bring forth more satisfactory confessions. To such as yielded readily to the admonitions of the Inquisitors, and, admitting the truth of the accusations against them, promised amendment for the future, absolution was generally accorded, on condition of performing penance.

This was of various degrees, according to the offence, involving a longer or lesser term of imprisonment, at the end of which the absolved were led forth from their dungeons clad in the sambenito, in which they were bound to stand at the doors of certain churches, and exposed to the revilings of the multitude. This process had to be repeated during a given period, and sometimes for life, from Sunday to Sunday, and on various festivals, and from time to time they had to listen to sermons in which the wickedness of their acts was portrayed in lively colours, and every exhortation to repentance was rehearsed.

The loss of their property was entailed on such as were more deeply dyed with infidelity, while to those who were more easily absolved a total or

partial restitution was conceded; but the adminis-
tration of the officials who were appointed to take
charge of the effects of prisoners, while undergoing
trial, was generally found to have ruined the estates,
and the less wealthy equally experienced that their
various industries had suffered, or had actually died
out. Thus the pardoned were returned to the world,
beggared in means of existence, and branded for
ever with the mark of heresy and infamy; moreover,
the withering glance of the Inquisition, like the
' evil eye ' of oriental superstition, was in future
always directed towards them, and tales of relapse
were easily invented and fastened on to those who
had once owned themselves guilty of the crime of
having wavered in their belief.

The tribunals of the Inquisition were as a rule
installed in stately, though generally gloomy, palaces,
where the Inquisitors, their secretaries, registrars,
and familiars were lodged in a becoming manner.
These buildings contained audience-chambers, halls
for the examination of prisoners and witnesses (who
were never allowed to be confronted together), and
also the prisons, which were of three kinds: the first
were denominated ' public,' and were intended for
such as, not having been guilty directly of crimes of
faith, were yet deemed legally amenable to the In-

quisition; the second were called 'intermediary,' and were reserved for such officers of the Holy Court as had misconducted themselves; and the third were the 'secret' cells, which formed the great bulk, being reserved for those who were accused of breaches of faith, and who had been condemned to incarceration for a term or for life.

These secret prisons were generally in the basement of the building, deep below the soil, dimly lighted, hardly ventilated, and reeking with filth, which was but rarely removed; sometimes the prisoner was solitary, sometimes four or five persons were thrust into the same narrow cell, about eight feet by six in size, where the fetid atmosphere, intense heat, and close confinement frequently generated fevers. Moreover, the food afforded to these unfortunate captives was of the coarsest and most unwholesome description; hard and mouldy bread and impure water, of which one jar only a week was supplied for all purposes, formed the staple of their diet, and when on rare occasions more generous food was allowed, it was frequently tainted, and hardly ever really nourishing.

Thus lodged and thus fed the prisoner might languish, neglected and forgotten, year after year, and many were the instances in which a prolonged incarceration, under these painful circumstances, finished by depriving the captive of his reason, leaving him to end his days in the condition of a brute. It was a frequent practice, when prisoners were awaiting further interrogation, to send persons into their cells under pretence of affording them consolation, but in reality to entice them into conversation, and thus to worm out, by means of unguarded expressions, proofs which might lead to their condemnation. Far away, in the remotest part of the building, was the subterranean chamber where torture was administered—a large bare vault, dimly lighted by lamps, and whose whole furniture consisted of a crucifix hung on the wall, and the grim apparatus of agony, under which the victim was to writhe. It is neither profitable, nor desirable, to dwell on the various modes of torture which the demoniacal ingenuity of one portion of our species has invented, in order to inflict suffering and agony on another.

In various times and countries we hear of the rack and the wheel, of thumb-screws, iron boots, collars and girdles of inverted nails, metal stools under which a slow fire was kindled, and similar atrocious engines, and as we gaze at these rusty emblems of infernal cruelty in various museums and collections, we shudder to think that men with minds similar to our own could have devised such horrors.

It is, however, proper to enumerate three special modes of torture, which were, it is said, devised by the Inquisition, and were certainly generally employed by it in addition to those instruments we have mentioned above. One was that by which the prisoner was drawn up by the hands by means of a pulley, cords being tied round his wrists, and heavy weights attached to his feet; when near the ceiling he was suddenly allowed to drop to within a few feet of the floor, by which awful shock his limbs were dislocated. This process was often repeated two or three times on the same individual. Another was the placing of the prisoner in a horizontal position, the middle of the body being slightly elevated above the extremities, and resting on an iron bar, and the head and feet being made fast by passing tight ropes round them; while thus held his nostrils were stopped, and his open mouth covered with a cloth, on which water was allowed to fall from a height, till it almost forced the cloth down his throat, when it was pulled out again, so as to allow respiration to return, and then the same proceeding was gone through over again. The third mode of torture was the strapping of the prisoner on the ground with his feet, which had been greased with lard, turned towards a roasting fire, in which position of agony he might be kept for an hour.

These tortures were administered by 'familiars' dressed in black, wearing mantles which covered their faces, holes being left for the eyes and mouth. Two Inquisitors were present to conduct the interrogation, and to take down the deposition of the accused. As may readily be supposed, very few could maintain their composure or their constancy under such terrible inflictions; maddened with agony the sufferers confessed to the most improbable, frequently impossible crimes, generally implicating by their incoherent statements as well friends and relations as many other persons whom they hardly knew. The next day, or as soon as the prisoner was sufficiently recovered, a copy of his confession was presented to him for ratification, and notwithstanding the falsity or absurdity of its various points, such was the fear of a repetition, or as it was called, 'continuation' of the torture, that it rarely happened that the prisoner failed to confirm his depositions. In those instances, where the accused recanted, the further application of torture was, as a rule, successful in wresting from him a full confirmation of all the previous statements, and usually much additional matter. In fact, courage and constancy availed nothing, as, in the parlance of the Inquisitors, these virtues were qualified as obduracy and impenitence, and those who displayed them were rewarded by being immured for years or for life in horrible dungeons, or were handed over to the secular arm, an euphemistic expression, which signified that the victims were to be sentenced to perish in the fires of an *auto-da-fé*, the Holy Court being too merciful itself to pronounce a sentence of death.

It is hardly remarkable that with so elaborate a process to criminate the accused, and with so little facility for establishing innocence, the instances of complete acquittal were so rare as hardly ever to occur, and it is reckoned that far less than one prisoner in a thousand left the walls of the Inquisition entirely unscathed, so that it became a proverb, 'A man may leave the Inquisition without being burned, but he is sure to be singed.'

Those condemned to form part of an *auto-da-fé* were kept imprisoned often for many years, till some grand festival, such as a coronation or a royal marriage, gave occasion for public rejoicing, when the grim spectacle was exhibited to the multitude of the faithful. An attempt must be made to describe this proceeding in order to give an idea of its full meaning.

G

About a month before the date appointed, generally
on a high festival, the announcement was made that
an *auto-da-fé* was fixed for a given date. The proclamation was made in grand state by the Inquisitor-
General with his numerous staff, his proud standard
of scarlet and gold floating before him, and amid an
array of troops in gay uniforms, and of priests and
monks in varied habits, with heralds accompanied
by a long procession of saints, images, relics, and
crucifixes glittering with precious stones, parading
the city amid cries of ‘Viva la fé!’ ‘the faith for
ever!’ The interval between the proclamation and
the execution was occupied in erecting, in the principal square or Plaza Mayor, the vast theatre for the
spectators and performers in the grand ‘Fiesta,’ as
it was called.

One of the most remarkable of these shows took
place in Madrid on Sunday, June 30, 1680, on the
occasion of the marriage of the almost demented
King, Charles II., then about twenty years of age,
with the Princess Marie Louise of Orleans, niece of
Louis XIV., the account of which, gathered from
various sources, by Kayserling and others, it may be
interesting to follow. An amphitheatre had been
constructed on the Plaza Mayor, with the box for the
King, Queen, and royal family on the one side, and

on the other a raised daïs for the Inquisitor-General, his superior officers, and the higher clergy. The ministers and Court officials in gala uniforms, and the various trade corporations in state dresses, with a motley group of monks in their respective habits, together with an overwhelming multitude of the populace, all assembled in the imposing arena, amid the pealing of bells and the chaunts of priests.

The ceremony began about six in the morning, and by eight, the King, Queen, Queen-mother, and Court, the foreign ambassadors with numberless ladies in Court dresses, and the innumerable dignitaries of the State, had taken the places reserved for them opposite the gallery of the Inquisitors, before which floated the green cross, the banner of the Holy office. The cry ' Viva la fé!' burst forth from myriads of throats, as the melancholy procession was seen entering the arena. A hundred charcoal-burners, clad in black, and armed with pikes and helmets, came first, as was their prescriptive right, they having furnished the wood for the sacrifice; then followed a number of Dominican monks, and the Duke of Medina Celi, hereditary standard-bearer of the Inquisition, with other friars and nobles bearing banners and crosses. Thirty-four images of life size, with their names inscribed in large letters,

and borne by the familiars of the Inquisition, represented those who had died in prison, or escaped by
flight; Dominican friars with coffins came next,
bearing the bones of those who had been convicted
of heresy after death, and then appeared fifty-four
men and women holding lighted tapers, and clad in
the sambenito and coroza, or high cap, almost all of
whom had been convicted of Judaising, but had
confessed and repented. Lastly followed eighteen
Jews and Jewesses, mostly persons of humble rank,
also wearing the sambenito and coroza, who were to
bear witness in the flames to their steadfastness to
the law of Israel. Most of them, haggard and worn
by long imprisonment, seemed languid and indifferent,
quite resigned to quit the world in which they had
suffered so intensely, but one beautiful girl about
seventeen, as she approached the royal stand, called
out, ' Noble queen, cannot your royal presence save
me from this? I sucked in my religion with my
mother's milk; must I now die for it?'

The young Queen's eyes filled with tears; she hid
her face, and the sad procession passed on. High
Mass was then celebrated before a grand altar, which
had been erected for the purpose, with all the pomp
which was thought befitting to the occasion. At
noon the Inquisitor-General with a staff of his

officials passed over to the King, with the Gospels in
his hands, upon which he administered to Charles
the oaths that he would support the faith and the
Inquisition, and do all that lay in him to extirpate
heresy. Next followed a sermon from one of the
principal chaplains of the King, Fray Tomas Navarro.
The text of this lengthy lecture which lasted a couple
of hours was, ' Arise, O Lord, and judge thy cause,'
and this was the refrain of the whole composition,
which from beginning to end was one vast tissue of
abuse of the Hebrew people, and one long string of
curses supported by passages from Scripture violently
wrested from their context. He adjured the Jews
before him to acknowledge the wickedness of their
ways, and to accept the doctrines of salvation before
that last moment of life, which was so painfully
drawing near. After this the prisoners were brought
to the staging, which had been erected in the middle
of the arena; each entered a sort of cage, and the
name of the individual, with the nature of the crimes
of which he or she was convicted, was read out in a
loud voice. The day was unusually sultry, but the
King sat out the fourteen hours without so much as
moving to take a mouthful of food.

Monks were continually hovering round the unfortunate Jews urging them to repent, and to acknow-

ledge their abominable heresy, but all in vain : the
harder the trial to which they were subjected, the
higher rose the heroism of these Hebrew men and
women, who were thus barbarously exposed like wild
beasts in the arena, when separated by but a few
hours from the most painful death. At length the
long-delayed shadows of this summer's eve drew on,
the evening Angelus pealed forth in its impressive
tones, vespers were grandly chaunted, absolution was
pronounced, and the Inquisitor leaving his throne
passed over to the King, when the fictitious ceremony
took place of handing over the prisoners to the secular
power, since the Church could not pronounce a ver-
dict of death. Then in the growing darkness was
organised the horrible procession to the Puerta
de Fuencarral, outside which was the Quemadero,
where the final scene was to take place. Those who
at the last moment confessed their penitence, had
the grace conceded to them of being strangled at the
foot of the pile ; the bodies of such, the bones of the
dead heretics, and the effigies of the absent were
first deposited at the stake, and lastly the living
victims, men and women, mounted the pile with so
firm a step that the chroniclers were fain to ascribe
their courage to some diabolical charm, in order not
to be forced to own their admiration. The King

himself kindled with his own hand the fatal pile, and soon the flames in which these noble beings perished mounted towards heaven amid the deafening plaudits of the multitude, and the whole city was lit up by the lurid light, which represented so vividly, as it was meant to represent, the flames of hell.

Those so-called penitents, who had life spared to live a life-long torment, were forced to assist at the horrible spectacle, after which they were taken back to their dungeons, which many of them were never to leave again, whilst others in a few days were sent off to the galleys.

Such were the scenes which with more or less similar circumstances were enacted in every large city in Spain, and Portugal, and in all the immense colonies, and dependencies of the two crowns. Sometimes twice or thrice in a year, sometimes not for several years together, depending much on the personal character of the sovereign, and still more on the greater or less degree of severity, which marked the Inquisitor-General. The monarchs of the Bourbon dynasty refused to be present at any *autos-da-fé*, and though one was celebrated on the accession of Philip V., in 1701, the King could not be persuaded to witness it; from this time the exhibition grew less frequent, and the last occasion on which a human being was burned alive in the name of the faith was at Seville in 1781, and the victim then was not a member of the Hebrew race.

In Portugal these human sacrifices did not survive so long, and although a grand *auto-da-fé* was celebrated in Lisbon in 1705, on which occasion the Archbishop of Cranganor delivered the voluminous and vituperative sermon, to which David Nieto, Chief Rabbi of the Jews in London, afterwards published a reply, the close of this long series of tragedies was not far distant. This took place in October 1739; the last sacrifice was an illustrious one, namely, Antonio José da Silva, a dramatic author of much merit, who was born in Brazil, to which country, taken from the Portuguese by the Dutch, and afterwards restored to the former, large numbers of converted Jews had flocked, and had there resumed their faith.

Antonio had been brought by his father, with the rest of his family, to settle in Lisbon; but it was not long before both father and son incurred the suspicion of the Inquisition, from the censures of which, however, they contrived to purge themselves. Da Silva henceforward led a secluded and literary life, enjoying the society of his young wife, and blessed with a little daughter, whose second birthday he was celebrating, when the familiars of the Holy Office pounced in upon the family circle, and hurried off him and his wife and mother to the dungeons of the Inquisition, upon the depositions of a negro maid-servant. After two years of painful confinement, and despite great interest exerted on his behalf, the young author was condemned to the flames, his wife and mother being sentenced to imprisonment as penitents, the latter surviving her son's sacrifice but three days.[1]

As may easily be imagined, many of the New

[1] The terrible earthquake of Lisbon, which happened on November 1st, 1755, and laid the greater part of the city in ruins, spreading death and desolation everywhere, and destroying between 30,000 and 40,000 of the inhabitants, proved the means of saving a considerable number of Jews from the jaws of the Inquisition. The palace of the Holy Court was overthrown in the common ruin, the walls of the prison house were violently split open, the gaolers fled for their lives, and such of the captives as escaped the general destruction, scared and horror-stricken, found themselves suddenly and fearfully restored to freedom. Bare of everything, and only possessed of the clothes they stood in, they lurked about among the smouldering ruins till they found, amid the general horror and consternation, a means of escape. Many of the New Christians thus freed managed to communicate with their families, and hastily collecting such valuables as were portable, and which were spared from the wreck of the earthquake, sought refuge on board the English and Dutch vessels in the harbour, meeting with a hospitable reception, and securing a passage to more tolerant lands. The Palace of the Inquisition in Lisbon seems never to have been rebuilt on the same scale as before, and its site is now occupied by the Great Theatre, in the Praza de Maria Segunda, commonly called the 'Rocio.'

Christians who still remained attached to Judaism sought, where possible, to effect their escape from Spain and Portugal to happier countries. Those who from force of circumstances, or from worldly considerations, remained behind, endeavoured by a public profession of Catholic orthodoxy, and the secret practice of Jewish ceremonies, to temporise between the loss of earthly possessions, or of life itself, and the sacrifice of every consideration, which their consciences held sacred. Many learned Jews sought refuge in the various Courts of Italy, where science and literature were specially cultivated. The distinguished family of the Usques were warmly received by the Duke of Ferrara, under whose patronage Abraham Usque published his translation of the Bible into Spanish—a work which had become very necessary, since the New Christians, being forced to abandon the study of Hebrew, were gradually losing all knowledge of the sacred language. Congregations of Spanish Jews were planted in Florence, Venice, and Leghorn, where their beautiful synagogue still attests no less their devotion than their wealth. The whole littoral of the Mediterranean, Morocco, Algiers, Tripoli, Tunis, Egypt, Syria, and the Turkish Empire, with the many islands of the Archipelago, became seats of Jewish industry, and to this day the Spanish language, full of antique forms, and written in Hebrew characters, constitutes the vernacular of hundreds of thousands of the descendants of the exiles throughout the whole of these countries.

Numbers found their way to the American colonies, whither the Inquisition followed them, so that they were forced to settle in the various territories and islands acquired by the Dutch and the English, where they openly re-assumed Judaism. A vast number established themselves in Holland, where, after its dearly-bought independence was established, a toleration, at first begrudged, was soon fully accorded to them. Here they founded synagogues, the first of which was opened in Amsterdam in 1598; here too they established charitable institutions and schools, and here they flourished during the seventeenth and eighteenth centuries in a remarkable degree. Some were allowed by Henry II. to settle in Bordeaux, Bayonne, and other towns in the south of France, and a few wandered into Hungary and the German Empire, thus reuniting themselves with the mass of their brethren, from whom they had for so many centuries been severed, and who had from time immemorial inhabited Central Europe, forming in this manner a slender chain between the Sephardim (Spanish Jews) of the East with those of Holland and the West.

The Dutch Republic became a second Spain to them, as Spain had been a second Judæa. Here the fugitives, freed from the horrible incubus of the In-quisition, threw off the hated garb of Catholicism, assuming Hebrew names in addition to those high-sounding family appellations with which they had been endowed by the noble Spaniards, who had stood sponsors for them at the font—the Alvarezes, the de Castros, the Mendozas, the de Souzas, the Aguilars, the d'Almeidas, the de Laras, the da Silvas, &c., all recalling the noblest names of Castilian and Lusi-tanian chivalry. Here they at once sought to be inducted into the practices and ceremonies of the Jewish religion, which generations of disguise had almost effaced from their recollection, and here they diligently studied the Hebrew language, to which they were entirely strangers.

Numbers of authors soon appeared, and a copious flow of elegant literature, in verse and in prose, chiefly bearing on religious subjects, generally in Spanish, sometimes in Portuguese, and occasionally in Hebrew, issued from the press. The Jews of Holland were eminently successful in pursuits of industry and commerce, by means of which large fortunes were accumulated, and important families were founded. The present splendid Portuguese synagogue of Amsterdam, bearing testimony to the importance of the congregation, was finished in 1660, four years prior to which date Manasseh ben Israel had obtained, from the Lord Protector, Cromwell, a somewhat informal permission for Jews to re-enter England, to which country many emigrated from Holland before the close of the century. Congregations were also formed in Hamburg and in Copenhagen, and the Spanish Jews, bearing with them their traditions, their industry and their wealth, together with the courtly bearing and gentle languages of the Peninsula, became diffused through all the leading centres of civilisation.

Among the many learned Jews who shone forth brilliantly amid the revived lustre of their community in Holland, one stands pre-eminent, namely, Baruch de Espinoza, better known as Benedict Spinoza, who was born in 1632, but whether in the Peninsula or in Amsterdam is not fully proved. This bold and profound philosopher, who had in early youth deeply studied the Hebrew writings, soon found the circle of Rabbinical reasoning too narrow for him, and after perfecting himself in Latin, he threw the whole force of his intellect into the rationalistic philosophy of Descartes. Boldly announcing his deistical, or rather pantheistical convictions, he entirely withdrew from the practices of Judaism, and though not adopting any other form of religion, he became so estranged from the Jews, to whom his philosophy was eminently distasteful, that a public ' Herem ' or excommunication was fulminated against him from the synagogue in 1656. Shunned by his own people, he pursued his studies in retirement, maintaining himself as an optician in the suburbs of Amsterdam, whence he afterwards withdrew, first to Leyden, and then to the Hague. His ' Principles of Philosophy,' in which he geometrically demonstrated the system of Descartes, whilst opening out a new and original field of metaphysics, aroused no less the wonder of the learned than the animadversions of the orthodox of every denomination. He afterwards published his ' Theologico-political Treatise,' and ' Metaphysical Meditations,' and shortly after his death appeared his posthumous works, including the celebrated treatise on ' Ethics, geometrically demonstrated.'

Throughout all his works Spinoza exhibited wonderful depth of thought and close reasoning, but, unfortunately, his propositions never lead up to any result of practical utility, since he always chose as the objects of his definitions those insoluble subjects, which are beyond all human comprehension—the Nature of the Deity, and the origin and destiny of man. Though in active correspondence with most of the greatest thinkers and many of the most illustrious personages of his day, he led a simple, obscure life. Never a strong man, and subjected to a moral persecution of the most galling kind, Spinoza died at the Hague in 1677, in the forty-sixth year of his age.

Many other distinguished men might be mentioned, most of whose writings display much elegance of style, and deep religious feeling, but we can hardly find space to dwell upon them here. The material substance of the Spanish Jews played a part in the history of the times almost as important as their mental superiority. Many of the most important transactions of the age were worked out by means of funds furnished by Jewish capitalists, and among the undertakings so helped is to be included the expedition of William of Orange, which placed him on the British throne.

In conclusion we must cast a lingering regard on those unfortunate Jews who still remained in the Peninsula under the name of New Christians. The Inquisition, as we have seen, continued its fell course, and sat as a ghastly incubus on the thoughts and actions of men. The unhappy Marannos, outwardly the most devout among the whole Catholic population, continued to follow out in the depths of secrecy the observances of the old faith, despite the excessive peril with which this course was fraught. Informers were so largely benefited by their delations, and suspicion was so easily aroused, that no man felt safe from the detractions of the servants of his household, from secret enemies, or from unguarded friends. The utmost caution hardly secured the New Christians from the suspicion of showing signs of a tendency towards Judaism. Their habits, dress, and especially diet, were carefully noted down; their abstention from or manner of performing any Catholic rite, their conduct on Jewish sabbaths and festivals, their very looks and gestures were diligently watched, and often the slightest unintentional action was reported on, and the grim familiars of the Holy Court were heard knocking at the door, ready to carry off their unsuspecting victim to its dungeons for months, for years, perhaps for ever.

Thus passed on generation after generation of secret Jews, mingling with every grade of society, and filling every office of the State, and more especially of the Church, living in constant fear and trembling, still steadfast at heart, and from time to time yielding their steady tribute to the dungeon and the stake. Partly from the aversion of the people to mingle their blood with that of 'the accursed seed of Israel,' partly from the desire of the Marannos themselves to keep alive the remembrance of Judaism in their progeny, the New Christians generally intermarried among each other; but many were the occasions in which the bluest blood condescended to ally itself with heiresses of Hebrew lineage, so that there were few among the noblest families of Spain and Portugal who did not derive descent from Jewish ancestors. To so great an extent was this the case, that, when Joseph, King of Portugal, asked his great Minister Pombal, in the middle of the last century, whether he could not devise a peculiar hat to be worn, as a distinguishing mark, by the New Christians, to keep them separate from persons of 'pure' blood, the great statesman brought three such hats to the king on the following day, and when asked for whom they were intended, he replied: 'The one is for the Inquisitor-General, another for myself, and the third for your Majesty,' thus indicating that Jewish blood flowed in the veins of all.

By means of constant emigration, however (and in 1629 a law was passed in Portugal, allowing secret

Jews to leave the country), by unrelenting persecution, by intermarriage, and by the natural consequences of separation from the rest of their brethren, the Jews assimilated more and more with the rest of the population. All through the last century families of New Christians, in groups or singly, continued to find their way out of the Peninsula, and, after two hundred and more years of disguise, openly resumed Judaism; even in our own times isolated examples of the same circumstance are known to have happened. Since the beginning of the present century foreign Jews have been permitted to settle in Portugal, and there are now synagogues in Lisbon and two or three other cities; the Portuguese Inquisition, however, was only formally abolished in 1821, although it had long become practically inoperative.

In Spain, Napoleon put an end to the Holy Court in 1808; it was reopened, however, when Ferdinand VII. was restored, and the reaction set in, but finally the Inquisition was closed, let us hope for ever, in 1820. At this day there are probably no secret Jews in Spain or Portugal, for though there are still remote parts of Andalusia, and certain districts, especially in the neighbourhood of Braganza, where the greater part of the population is known to be of Jewish origin, and where still some lingering traditions of Hebrew observances can be traced, the meaning of such practices has now become lost, and they are merely recognised as customs of unknown significance handed down from preceding generations. Jews who settle in Spain are in these days in no way interfered with; but the establishment of a synagogue has not as yet been attempted, and would probably not be allowed, as, despite certain vague clauses in the constitution enjoining toleration, the spirit of the Inquisition still lingers in the minds of the people, and the edict of Ferdinand and Isabella has never been formally repealed.

LONDON : PRINTED BY
SPOTTISWOODE AND CO., NEW-STREET SQUARE
AND PARLIAMENT STREET